YOUNG PEOPLE AS CITIZENS NOW

towards more inclusive and coherent policies for young people

The report of a non-aligned working group following a consultation on youth policy at St George's House, Windsor Castle.

Printed by

17–23 Albion Street, Leicester LE1 6GD.
Tel: 0116.285.6789. Fax: 0116.247.1043.
Information Centre Minicom: 0116.247.1043.

© Members of the Working Group March 1997
£6.50
ISBN 0 86155 183 4

Y O U T H • W O R K • P R E S S
is a publishing imprint of the National Youth Agency

The views expressed in this book are those of the Working Group and do not
necessarily represent the views of the National Youth Agency.

Contents

Foreword

Sir Geoffrey Holland KCB

OUR HOPE for the future rests with our young people, as it always has done. Yet for each generation there is a new context with new challenges, and we and our young people live and in reality are partners in the present.

In this country, it has not been our custom to develop and implement coherent youth policies through single structures at central or local level. However, in an ever changing moral, social and economic world with pressures from many lobbies, the interests of young people can become, and perhaps have become over recent decades too marginal for the national good. Certainly there is now recognition by many adults that their children and grandchildren are likely to have less opportunity, in particular less job security and all that goes with it, than they did themselves. Young people are keenly aware of this also. We live in a world of global trade and competition, with increasing output of talent and skills in many countries whose educational systems were founded well after our own.

This report has been triggered by one aspect of the work of St George's House, a unique study centre within Windsor Castle which endeavours to serve the nation and its churches in response to changing circumstances. I hope that the report will be widely read and debated within youth agencies, local communities and those parts of central and local government which have responsibilities for optimising the talents and commitment to citizenship of our young people.

What counts for young people is of course their own life experience and what they make of it. There are obviously limits to the

Summary

THIS REPORT IS the product of a small, experienced, yet independent Working Group. The Working Group believes that the report speaks for the hopes of many young people aged from 13 to 25. It also details the experiences of those who work with them in communities and further afield. The broad context in which youth issues are raised is described. Particular emphasis is given to the challenges and risks, for many young people, of a varied and drawn out contemporary phase of transition into adult life. Based on fresh soundings of a number of young people and those who help to develop them, the report articulates some clear core principles for youth policy and the means by which they can be implemented.

Recommendations centre around five main themes:

1 The need for a coherent national youth policy, along with efficient structures and mechanisms for its delivery nationally (including an executive Youth Affairs and Services Agency), as well as regionally and locally.

2 The requirement for those with influence to listen to what young people are saying about their lives and their legitimate wishes for genuine and wide-ranging civic participation.

3 The urgent need to make education more relevant and flexible to life's demands, capturing more of the potential enthusiasm of young people by creative teaching approaches, and giving far greater emphasis towards coherent personal, relationship and citizenship education.

proposals, in practice, may exhibit some variations.

The youth field is far from short of reports, and in much that we have compiled there is no claim to originality. That we believe is a strength, for we have endeavoured to stand on others' shoulders where appropriate, as reflected in the bibliographic references. What we have tried to do is take a fresh look and emphasise some perspectives which we believe have been neglected in the past.

The report was previewed and generally well-received at a short consultation at St George's House attended by senior members of youth services on 6-7 November 1996. A number of minor revisions have been made subsequently, largely in order to clarify two of the key proposals. The Working Group was grateful to Mr James Paice MP, Parliamentary Under-Secretary of State in the Department for Education and Employment, for attending as a keynote speaker at that event and providing an initial response to our proposals.

I take this opportunity to thank my co-members of the Working Group and the assessor. We have pushed each other, amid many other responsibilities, at a speed which the topic merits. The sudden death of Mary Tuck two days prior to our final meeting was a deep shock to us; it will be a fitting tribute to her wisdom, and compassion for young people, if this report does more than gather dust.

Richard Whitfield
Chairman of the Working Group
(Warden of St George's House and Emeritus Professor of Education at the University of Aston)
Windsor Castle, January 1997
Tel: 01753 861341

Membership of the Working Group

Gabriella Civico, Chair, British Youth Council
(Rev) Don Coleman, Director, Royal Philanthropic Society
Ian Pawlby, Head of the Youth Exchange Centre, The British Council
The late **Mary Tuck**, Retired Head of Research, The Home Office
Professor Richard Whitfield, Warden of St George's House
(Chairman)
Tom Wylie, former HMI and now Chief Executive of the National Youth
Agency
Assessor: **Graham Holley**, Head of the Youth Service and Preparation
for Adulthood Division, Department for Education and Employment.

Simon Richey, Assistant Director (Education) at the Gulbenkian
Foundation also attended most sessions of the Working Group which
usually met at that Foundation's London offices.

Grant aid, held on trust by St George's House, to meet the costs of the
Working Group and of the report and appropriate later debate was
gratefully received from the Royal Philanthropic Society, The
Gulbenkian Foundation and the Department for Education and
Employment.

part that public policies can play in that, and perhaps fortunately so. The local contexts of home and community clearly play a crucial role in shaping daily life and opportunity even in the television and video age. What informed policy discussion can do is create a climate and shift priorities and therefore values. This report should be read and discussed in that light. I hope it will lead to new action growing from the best of our present and past practices.

Sir Geoffrey Holland KCB
Vice-Chancellor, University of Exeter
(Formerly Permanent Secretary at the Departments for Education and Employment, and Head of the Manpower Services Commission)

Preface

Professor Richard Whitfield

O
UR WORKING GROUP, and the resources to service it, arose as a
consequence of a Consultation on Youth Policy held at St George's
House in November 1995. During that event it became clear that the
traditional patchwork of provision of services and opportunities for
young people had become threadbare, at least in parts, failing to include
a sufficiently high proportion of young people to assist them in their
transition to adulthood as family members and as citizens. Many of the
consultation participants, reflecting a broad range of youth interests in
the UK, felt that a nationally sensitive independent report could be timely
if it were produced prior to a 1997 General Election.

This report is the result of carrying forward those sentiments. The
Working Group has taken appropriate soundings within a short
timescale. While recognising the difficulties of achieving far more
coherent youth policies, the Working Group is unanimous in urging a
range of strategic changes and shifts of investment in order to increase
the sense of security and civic purpose of many young people in need or
at risk of further social alienation. Some of our proposals will be seen as
controversial. We wish to encourage vigorous debate about them, for
there is a need for change and reform on more than a piecemeal basis.

The focus of this report is on issues affecting young people which
are perceived to be of national significance. At the same time, we
recognise that there are clearly some regional variations on these issues
and, in addition, structures are unique to each region. However, we
believe that the principles contained in this report will be equally
relevant to all regions of the UK, although the application of these

4 A new deal on jobs and work experience for young people which involves the cultural reconceptualisation of employment, and provides for clear and guaranteed options within a new national scheme of carefully supervised Civic Service Work (CSW). CSW would be available to all young people at the earliest appropriate time, but before the age of 25, and encompass many options with a total full-time equivalent commitment of between 6 and 12 months.

5 A realignment of national priorities as policies are constructed in a variety of fields so that they are 'proofed' with respect to young people and parents who are supporting them to promote home stability, social inclusion, opportunity, civic pride and responsibility.

The Working Group hopes that its report will be widely discussed and acted upon at a range of levels. Given the support of all political parties and the voluntary sector, we can create a new social dynamic for and covenant with young people as we work together today to shape tomorrow's world. The alternative combination of incoherence and relative indifference with respect to youth's voice and desire for involved citizenship already has high social and economic costs. In essence, a coherent youth policy requires a new compact between the generations.

Chapter 1

Background to and structure of the report

'Adults are the bows from which children and youth are sent forth as living arrows'
(adapted from Kahlil Gibran's *The Prophet*)

A RE WE SATISFIED with the formation, character, competence and skills of the young whom we are sending forth as 'living arrows' to be the guardians of tomorrow's world? Have we in our generation given them a world fit to inherit, not only as consumers, but as creative, purposeful whole persons? Are we staying close enough to them to enable the shaping of their identities amid sufficient security?

These seem to us to be fair questions. Nonetheless they make us feel uncomfortable. Even when our own imperfect beginnings are taken into account, for we all have an inheritance of many dimensions, we sense that our society collectively can and should do better for many of our young people. The strong message from a range of available data shows that it is they who have borne and are bearing a disproportionate share of the burdens of changes in family order, gender relations, economic and labour market transformation, global capital movements and the information and media revolutions. Their childhood platform for young personhood and then adulthood has not been shaped in normal evolutionary times. We have under-invested in them, not least of our time in interaction in home and community. There is now good reason to believe that, proportionately, national fiscal resources have in recent years been slipping away from young people, broadly viewed in this report as 13 to 25-year-olds.

We do not have simplistic solutions to the many problems of youth, intensified particularly we believe for this generation both psychologically and practically. However, we are sure that youth issues will not rise within national priorities without measured advocacy and the shaping of and investment in a number of strategic youth policies. These must be able to command wide public backing and extend from the best of long-standing and newer good practice with and for young people. Our report builds in that direction.

The professional context for the report originated in two separate consultations held at St George's House, Windsor, involving about seventy widely experienced participants. The first of these took place in March 1994 within a series on family policy and focused upon 'Young People's Transition to Independence: The Leaving Home Process'. The second, held in November 1995, was devoted specifically to an overview of youth policy.

From their differing perspectives each of the consultations, involving a broad range of participants concerned for and with young people – researchers, advisers, administrators and fieldworkers, and some young people – developed significant solidarity of view. There was broad agreement concerning the analysis and interpretation of the status and circumstances of young people in contemporary society, and about a number of options for priority attention within public policy involving both the state and voluntary sectors. Both consultations, upon sober reflection on the digests of evidence and experience presented in plenary sessions and group discussions, developed a clear sense of urgency concerning the need to tackle some key structural and practical issues. Too high a proportion of young people are unanchored, unable to find a sufficient sense of purpose and confidence to make constructive contributions to their society as young citizens.

For example, the key overall 'finding' from the first consultation was that:

> *'society has a lack of respect for young people, thus creating excessive intergenerational tensions'.*

The broad response to this was seen to be through:

> *'a serious national interdepartmental strategic youth policy, with local sensitivity … along with high status, personal and social education at all stages of the youth developmental process'.*

The second consultation, presented with some different yet complementary perspectives, resolved to take this proposed response further forward against the revealed background of relative priority indifference within political parties. For example, one suggestion was that all public policies should be 'youth-proofed' in terms of potential impacts. Work was also done on a draft *Young Person's Charter* (see Appendix C, page 85) and, alongside that, on the fundamental principles of youth policy (see Chapter 5, page 45). Her Royal Highness the Princess Royal (who attended two sessions of the second consultation) had suggested that those principles appeared to lack clarity among those working with young people let alone for the general public. This consultation viewed unanimously the development of youth policy, and the practice which would flow from it 'as an urgent national social issue'.

In essence that was the Working Group's starting point. Within it 'youth' is perceived as a relatively distinctive group with particular developmental tasks of transition to adulthood, and a need to have enriching opportunities for participation in civic life. These are what social anthropologists have long termed rites of passage within human needs over the life course; in all coherent societies such rites have been safeguarded by 'tribal' customs and 'policies'.

While of course young people are all individuals with a wide range of aspirations and interests, they are moving through the 'in-between' stage between childhood and adulthood. This has for many become elongated as a result of socio-economic changes, including often more exacting labour market demands. An infant or child is not an adult, while a young person is in transition between those two practical states (see Chapter 3, page 31). Therefore we believe that as a distinctive, special, though varied group, youth needs, no less than senior citizens, a range of interlinked and responsive public policies.

However, we do not see youth for the most part as a victim culture; rather as an insufficiently understood and somewhat neglected segment of society in whom our future hope simply has to be seriously invested. We are concerned here with mainstream youth, and not simply marginal groups, for alienation and disaffection are risks to which all can fall prey.

This report draws on the two consultations referred to, but is enhanced by data from further soundings of both young people and professional informants in the voluntary and statutory sectors. Outlined in Chapter 4 is evidence from young people gathered during a 24-hour residential consultation with representatives from a handful of localised youth councils in the north and south of England and Scotland. Also in Chapter 4 are some findings drawn from a brief postal questionnaire which was distributed to a range of youth organisations.

The pattern of the report moves from considering many of the risks and challenges which beset youth today, including the transition to adult life, to some core principles for youth policy duly informed by our soundings and experience. These then provide a platform for a policy action map in terms of topic content, mechanisms to make it work and obstacles which do or might undermine its fulfilment. Finally, we lay out some broad yet clear recommendations which have wide yet achievable implications.

Chapter 2

Why youth policy matters: the context

MANY QUALIFIED analysts have noted that we do not live in 'normal' evolutionary times. At the most optimistic, our culture is in a state of highly unstable equilibrium. There are many reasons, among which are:

- the pace of change and our problematic adaptation to it as a long evolved species;
- the very partial paradigms of materialist, scientific and economic determinism which drive the dominant culture and tend to diminish other forms of human capability, awareness and insight into the human condition;
- global competition and mass communications; and
- a somewhat pervasive moral relativism, which can disrespect full personhood and human vulnerability in community, and has contributed to a range of confusions about guidance and authority.

Some would also wish to emphasise the neglect of spiritual development, viewed as a far wider concept than organised religion. Much scientific evidence and individual testimony keeps alive the proposition that humankind is on Planet Earth other than by mindless chance, a 'reality' which manifestly sustains a sense of civic purpose and personal meaning for many.

Such factors have increasingly crystallised practically in the breakdown of implicit trust between the generations, reflected most in the decay of family solidarity and stability. At root this is the consequence of major forces in society becoming implicitly cavalier about the optimum conditions for begetting and then raising babies, infants, children and adolescents through sufficient attention to their care, control and development. The structure of the labour market and the collapse of 'the family wage' is a key factor in this. Parental time in interaction with the young is at a premium even in the two-parent intact family, and there is often a false presumption that adolescents need less parental time and appropriate supervision than do pre-school and primary school children. The human species needs active, involved and preferably insightful, sensitive parenting, and in contemporary society for the order of two decades.

Here it is not appropriate to go into the detail of the social context for young people's growing up. Instability in relationships is a key factor as shown by a range of indicators, and, since humans are social animals, such tendencies are broadly disabling to all parties, and not least dependants. Certainly, the need for youth policies has become heightened as a result of adult relational instability and its frequently negative impacts upon parental roles and capabilities. As we will note later, youth policies cannot be dissociated from appropriate help and support for parents of teenagers and young adults, an area of great neglect.

By and large young people growing up are still exercised with the basic necessities of life – getting on with others, finding an opportunity to work or study, eventually somewhere to live and an income which will sustain them as independent adults. These outcomes help young people make the transition into adulthood. But they have become markedly more difficult to achieve and for a significant number they remain elusive. Policies to facilitate the process of transition are having an uneven and sometimes negative impact. With the overall trend towards fewer opportunities in the labour market for early school-leavers (i.e. 16 to 18-year-olds) there is now an increasingly lengthy period before full adult status is achieved, with major implications for education and training beyond about the age 14.

Living without the rhythm of work, a regular income and the certainty of a place to live is unsettling. Inevitably it affects other aspects of young people's lives – relationships and health also suffer, studying becomes more difficult. Crime, alcohol, and drugs become more attractive as sources of quick money and forms of escape. Future prospects for forming a new stable home base from which to partner and to parent, for those who so choose, become markedly diminished.

Figure 1: Youth contexts and risks

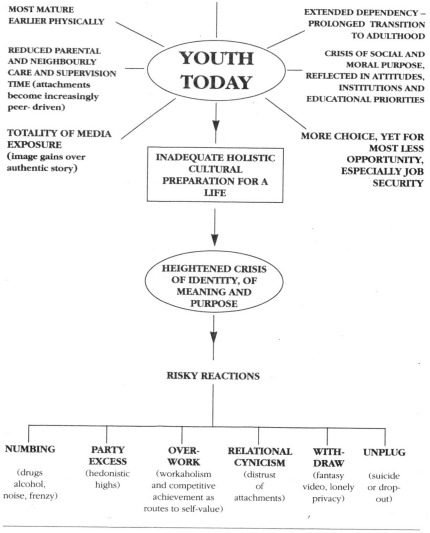

UNSTABLE & IMCOMPLETE
FAMILY STRUCTURES –
PARENTAL STRESS AND DISTRESS
(risks to attachment, trust and security,
with imperfect safety nets)

MOST MATURE
EARLIER PHYSICALLY

REDUCED PARENTAL
AND NEIGHBOURLY
CARE AND SUPERVISION
TIME (attachments
become increasingly
peer- driven)

TOTALITY OF MEDIA
EXPOSURE
(image gains over
authentic story)

EXTENDED DEPENDENCY –
PROLONGED TRANSITION
TO ADULTHOOD

CRISIS OF SOCIAL AND
MORAL PURPOSE,
REFLECTED IN ATTITUDES,
INSTITUTIONS AND
EDUCATIONAL PRIORITIES

MORE CHOICE, YET FOR
MOST LESS
OPPORTUNITY,
ESPECIALLY JOB
SECURITY

YOUTH TODAY

INADEQUATE HOLISTIC
CULTURAL
PREPARATION FOR A
LIFE

HEIGHTENED CRISIS
OF IDENTITY, OF
MEANING AND
PURPOSE

RISKY REACTIONS

NUMBING	PARTY EXCESS	OVER-WORK	RELATIONAL CYNICISM	WITH-DRAW	UNPLUG
(drugs alcohol, noise, frenzy)	(hedonistic highs)	(workaholism and competitive achievement as routes to self-value)	(distrust of attachments)	(fantasy video, lonely privacy)	(suicide or drop-out)

Figure 1 shows a summary of the context and risks associated with contemporary youth. Implicit is severe criticism of the cultural preparation of young people for shaping a full life, The multiple 'risky reactions' which deliberately do not mention crime specifically (though that is a serious issue for all too many young people), are reason alone for having preventative youth policies in place, aside from addressing the wider structural factors concerning jobs, gainful leisure and education in particular as both a preparative and redressive tool.

We cannot review here the extensive contemporary literature of the education and training industry. The same applies to the employment market, the benefits system, housing, health, crime and leisure. Our object is to highlight the main *contextual issues* which point to the need for an improved and extended range of youth policies.

Education

A major national policy preoccupation is Britain's economic competitiveness with other nations in Europe, North America and the 'tiger economies' of the Pacific Rim. It is inevitable that a consequent concern is for the quality of the UK's labour force and hence of its educative and training systems. The CBI commented in 1995:

> *The UK's performance at producing higher level students is comparable to its competitor nations. However, at the lower levels, the UK fails to match other countries' abilities to produce large numbers of medium-skilled students. Too many students in the UK leave school with low-level or no qualifications.'*

Similar perspectives are evident in the most recent White Paper on competitiveness. Over the last decade there has been a sharp rise – some 20 percentage points – in the numbers of those who stay on in education after 16, although substantial numbers drop away in subsequent years and a greater proportion of girls than boys remain in full-time education. There have been similar gains too, in the proportions gaining GCSEs, Scottish standard and higher grades, and A-levels. But direct comparisons of educational performance at school level consistently show UK pupils performing relatively poorly in comparison with other leading European and Pacific economies. Differences in educational performance tend to be for most students strongly linked to social and economic background, including parenting variables. Nonetheless the nature of educational provision and the skills of teachers make measurable differences, though less than could be the case if serious investments were made in homes and communities as educators.

Almost one in three young people now enter higher education, compared with one in seven in 1987. There are now approximately 1.3 million undergraduate and postgraduate students in higher education, with two-thirds studying full-time. Almost 184,000 students graduated in England in 1995, over 100 per cent more than in 1985, and Britain has the second highest graduation rate in the European Union. But the proportion of students dropping out of university rose by 10 per cent between 1993–94 and 1994–95, while the number of those leaving after failing their exams rose by 20 per cent. About 60 per cent of the 54,000 HE students who left early did so for non-academic reasons, a fact which probably merits further enquiry.

Over the ten years from 1984, the proportion of those aged 16+ in full-time education increased more rapidly in the further education sector than in schools but a concern remains about the wide range of FE courses on offer, their relative value and high levels of drop out. The value of discretionary awards for students on FE courses has fallen. Students studying in FE colleges are also restricted in the social security benefits they can claim.

In England and Wales annual HE maintenance awards for students living away from home outside London for the 1994–95 academic year were £2,265. In the 1995–96 year the average debt applying to over half a million students after three years of study was over £1,200, and this is widely expected to rise over the next few years well beyond inflation. Given little formal educational attention to the art of effective personal financial management, including its underpinning values, society is conditioning many young people to mortgage their own future, a fact which looks likely to affect the formation of the next generation of families among other things.

Growing numbers of pupils are excluded from school – for example, a four-fold increase in the under 12s between 1991 and 1995. Worsening behaviour of pupils, changes in the procedures for exclusion, devolution of responsibility to schools and an increasingly competitive ethos between schools, rising class sizes, and changing attitudes to behaviour are among the explanations given. Young Black people are disproportionately affected by school exclusion. Bullying has become a more publicly acknowledged issue in recent years. Research shows strong positive attitudes towards education but there are marked gender, ethnic and school differences. Girls are now significantly outshining boys in many areas of performance, arguably a reflection of the comparative insecurities of contemporary male identity and almost certainly requiring specific cultural responses for young males.

Training

The Government's intention is to encourage lifetime learning and it is particularly concerned that young people who leave school at 16 should continue in educational training until the age of 18 or 19 through its YT guarantee and the FEFC duty. From the mid 1970s, the development of national training strategies has been closely linked with increasing levels of unemployment. There has been some tension in the goals of programmes. The Government's intention has been to provide high-quality training in the form of NVQs and to expand the skills base upon which the future success of the economy is seen to depend. Others have sometimes wondered if some programmes have effectively only provided a containing mechanism for the young unemployed.

The proportion and total number of 16 to 17-year-olds entering youth training has fallen steeply in recent years, though it is predicted to rise again. Nearly 270,600 young people were in Youth Training (including Youth Credits) in Great Britain in August 1995. In 1994, 12 per cent of those who had finished compulsory education entered YT, compared with 24 per cent in 1989. Nonetheless, the intention is for young people to have a choice of options available to them at 16; motivational factors, derivative from earlier educational and social experience, are often a problem.

From the start of YT some 10 per cent of young people were estimated to have rejected the schemes on offer, even after Income Support was withdrawn. Of those who enrol for YT 44 per cent drop out before the end of the course; some of those do so in order to enter employment. Of those who complete their YT courses, three-quarters gain a qualification, or a credit towards one, and about half of YT completers go into full-time employment (although only a third of young Black trainees do so). A recent research study commissioned by the Training and Enterprise Councils suggested that substantial numbers were dissatisfied with their experiences in YT and the lack of subsequent job prospects. Many others have no doubt benefited.

The Government offers some financial incentives for young people to continue in full-time education or job training. However, people under 18 are now unable to claim Income Support. Instead they are guaranteed a place on the YT scheme which, at 16, attracts a minimum weekly payment of £29.50 and £35.00 at 17. The YT allowance for 16-year-olds has been frozen since 1979. However, Income Support/Housing Benefit is available for those in training or waiting for a YT place who are categorised as being in genuine need. Also, some young people in training have their allowances topped-up by employers or are paid wages as employees. Clearly the real prize is a timely and relevant qualification that will bring its own rewards in terms of a worthwhile career and the likelihood or possibility of higher pay in the future.

In December 1996, the Government published its strategy for the education and training of 14 to 19-year-olds in the White Paper *Learning to Compete*. This includes a range of measures aimed at improving the country's skill base and offering a wide range of opportunities tailored to the needs and aptitudes of young people. For example, from September 1997 National Traineeships will be offered which will build on the success of Modern Apprenticeships to help 16 to 19-year-olds reach NVQ Level 2 and to acquire key skills.

Employment

All sectored comments on the labour market have to be prefaced with the fact that there is presently rapid change.

Young people aged 16 to 24 make up 17 per cent of the workforce today, compared with 23 per cent in 1986. This change is influenced by a fall in the total number of young people in this age band and a greater proportion of them staying on in full-time education.

Sales, personal and clerical occupations provide half of all jobs for under 25s. Young people in work are concentrated in sales and personal services occupations, chiefly in the distribution, hotel and catering industries, and are often part-time employed. The proportion of 16 to 24-year-old men in temporary jobs is more than four times as high than for 25 to 55-year-olds.

The unemployment rate among economically active 16 to 19-year-olds is 19.5 per cent and 13 per cent for those aged 20 to 24. Unemployment rates among young people under 25 have risen by about a quarter since 1990 and by a similar fraction for 16 to 17-year-olds during the 1995–96 year when there were otherwise promising signs of general economic recovery.

Under 25s account for more than one in four of all those unemployed and claiming benefit, and one in six of all long-term unemployed claimants. There were over six hundred thousand aged under 25 claiming benefit in the UK in October 1995, nearly a quarter of whom had been without work for 12 months or more; such long-term unemployment has increased by 75 per cent since 1990.

Without a job, and breaking into the labour market is a tough key hurdle, most young adults lack an anchor in their lives and their self-esteem is impaired. Programmes need to address the attitudinal and social problems which long-term unemployment can bring. Without work many young people also find themselves dependent on their parents or friends, and this in turn delays independence.

While young people have been bearing a disproportionate burden of unemployment, their average levels of pay have also declined proportionately compared with adults as shown in Table 1.

Table 1: Young People's Earnings as a percentage of Average Adult Earnings

Year		1985	1995	Decline %
Age under 18	*males*	37	31	6
	females	52	44	8
Age 21 to 24	*males*	76	69	7
	females	89	79	10

Apart from the limited incomes which young people in low paid work receive, an additional effect is that those who earn less than the National Insurance threshold (currently £58) lose their rights to a number of social security benefits, including unemployment benefit, state pension, statutory sick pay and statutory maternity pay.

Benefits

The underlying trend over the past 20 years, and especially since 1988, has been to reduce the range and level of social security benefits paid to young people. The policy position appears to be that young people out of the labour market either have lower needs than older people or should be financially dependent on their parents. The critical defining point for being free of such dependency is increasingly 25 years, and implies an extension of parental duties which many appear to be unable to fulfil. Hence, for example, it has been observed that:

> *'There are many cases of young people who are forced out of the family home because they have no income and their parents cannot afford to keep them. This is completely contrary to the intention of current Government policy. Such young people are often left destitute and on the streets because of the inadequacy of the benefit safety net.'*
> (Briefing, *Coalition on Young People and Social Security*, January 1995)

In place of a benefit safety net, Government has provided a guaranteed place on YT which attracts the living allowances noted in the Training section above. Apart from this there is a system of Income Support and Bridging Allowances which have complex criteria for their application. Each year since 1992 over a hundred thousand unemployed 16 to 17-year-olds not in education or training appear to have been left without any legitimate personal income. This represents over 80 per cent in that category (85 per cent in 1995) who, in the absence of strong parental emotional and financial support, are clearly a significant at risk group. Some are no doubt living at home, with their parents claiming child benefit, waiting to take up a suitable training place. Others clearly have no viable family bonds, let alone a focused motivation to take up a training place.

In 1996 Unemployment Benefit and Income Support were replaced by the Jobseeker's Allowance. As a result from October 1996, 18 to 24-year-olds who become unemployed will receive 20 per cent less benefit than those aged 25 and over regardless of their National Insurance contributions record.

Housing and Homelessness

Almost two-thirds of 16 to 24-year-olds live with their parents, 13 per cent live in privately rented accommodation, 13 per cent are owner occupiers, 7 per cent live in local authority accommodation and 2 per cent live in housing association properties. The Office of Population, Censuses and Surveys estimated that the number of under-25s living alone will increase by almost 30 per cent between 1991 and 2011.

The average age for leaving home is 21 for men and 20 for women. However, the number of young people returning home for significant periods of time has increased since the mid 1980s, with almost a third of young people doing so at some point. But 13 per cent of young people have left home by the age of 16 and a third have gone by the age of 19. The figures for young people in care are much higher – 28 per cent leave at 16 and 31 per cent at 17.

There are no official statistics on youth homelessness in Britain. Most young single homeless people are not considered by local authorities to fall within their statutory housing duties, so that insights in this important area come from scattered sources.
For example:

- Survey of hostel residents outside London: 44 per cent under 26, 8 per cent under 18 (Association of Metropolitan Authorities).
- Over 40 per cent of those being helped by the London-based youth homelessness charity Centrepoint are 17 and under.
- Over a quarter of single people living rough, or living in hostels and bed and breakfast accommodation, are 16 to 24-year-olds (Department of the Environment, 1993).
- Between 20 per cent and 50 per cent of the young homeless (and a third of the prison population) have been in care.

CHAR, a housing campaign group, estimated that in 1994 there were over a hundred thousand single young homeless people in England and Wales in the age band 16 to 25, while the new and more reliable estimate of the National Enquiry into Youth Homelessness (October 1996) provides a figure of a little over a hundred and forty thousand for urban districts of over a quarter of a million population alone. The health, employability and crime implications of this problem are significant.

Clearly the situation of young people with respect to housing has, aside from family circumstances, a wider context. A crucial factor, according to housing organisations, is the drop in suitable accommodation since local authorities sold off their council houses to private buyers. This generated a shortfall in housing stock, particularly in social housing for people on low incomes, or for those who for personal reasons need special accommodation.

Health

Accidents are the largest single cause of death for all ages up to 30. The rate of accidents increases four-fold between 15 to 24 years, traffic accidents being particularly significant. Risk-taking and experimentation is often seen as a key feature in adolescence as part of the quest for identity and social adjustment. There are often strong peer influences, in particular experimentation with drugs, sex and alcohol.

Sexual health is one of several key areas identified by the Government in its Health of the Young Nation campaign. Launched in July 1995, it aims to reduce the rate of conception for girls aged 13 to 15 by 50 per cent by the year 2000. Around eight thousand girls under 16 become pregnant each year and half have their pregnancies terminated, figures which do not compare favourably with other European countries. Sexually transmitted diseases are another key concern, particularly gonorrhoea and HIV infection: 18 per cent of HIV-1 infections have been from the 18 to 24 age group.

Suicide rates, particularly for young men whose incidence is treble that for females, have shown a steady increase in the past 20 years. This is the second most common cause of death for those aged 15 to 19, with the rate doubled over the past 20 years. It has been estimated that about

20 per cent of children and young people need help with some form of mental health problem. Depression and obsessive compulsive and eating disorders make up the major problems, having no doubt complex patterns of causation.

Drug and alcohol abuse are major health concerns. Accurate figures are hard to obtain as most drug use is illegal. Research suggest that some 40 per cent of 16 to 24-year-olds have taken some form of illegal drug, usually cannabis. The number of younger notified addicts is increasing, and in 1995 over a third of individuals presenting to drug agencies were under 25. Alcohol abuse is on the increase. By 14 the vast majority of teenagers have tried alcohol, with regular drinking becoming common between the ages of 14 to 17.

Smoking remains a significant health problem for young people with regular smokers making approximately 10 per cent of 11 to 15-year-olds. There is also concern about obesity and lack of physical exercise among increasing numbers of young people, with long-term health implications and costs.

Crime, including protective factors

Crime is a matter of national concern and young people are often the focus of attention. Youth convictions have been steadily dropping since the early 1990s. For example, 132,800 young adults were found guilty of or cautioned for indictable offences in 1981 compared with 90,500 in 1993. Self-report figures, however, indicate that law-breaking among young people is a common occurrence: one in two males and one in three females admit to having committed offences at some time.

The vast majority of crimes committed by young people involve burglary and theft. Violent crime is relatively small. For recorded offences the peak ages for offending are 18 and 15 for males and females respectively: self-report figures place the peak ages higher. Young people also make up a significant number of the victims of crime. A very small percentage of young people appear to commit a disproportionate volume of offences. Females aged 14 to 17 are nearly as likely as males to be involved in offending, but as they get older, this practice drops off sharply in comparison with males.

Criminological studies of youth give us good insights into precursors of succumbing to certain behavioural risks and getting found out. These also have implications for our understanding of risky behaviours not classified as criminal. There is a range of strongly indicative findings from many studies. Briefly, key determinants of youth crime are:

- insecure attachment relationships with parents;
- lone parenthood, or dysfunctional step-parenthood, with boys being particularly vulnerable to absent fathers;
- low parental supervision and low parental interaction time;
- peer friends in trouble with the police; and
- unsatisfactory leaving home processes.

Social class and material deprivation are generally not the overriding variables. Secure attachments to parent figures are gifts which cannot be purchased, and there is much affluent emotional neglect with consequences only partially reflected in crime studies.

Longitudinal studies show that much juvenile crime can be reasonably well predicted by the age of 8, with school truancy later emerging as significant. The sense of maternal well-being (i.e. mothers not depressed or without personally validating support) during the first years of life is a strong earlier indicator.

Correspondingly, protective factors against offending and risky behaviours are:

- attachment to family and general contentment at home;
- intact family structure;
- avoidance of drug use and bad company;
- successful transition to young adulthood by respectively leaving home, having a job, an adequate place to live and stable new relationships;

And, interestingly in recent British work:

- coming from an Asian household.

Why young people stop offending is related to major life events characterising the transition from childhood to adulthood (see Chapter 3, page 31). These include completing full-time education, taking up stable employment, leaving home, getting married/forming a stable partnership, looking after children and taking responsibility for themselves and others. On the basis of these criteria, many young people are clearly not completing the transition to adulthood by the age of 25, with, on all these measures, males lagging behind females.

Males stop offending more gradually and intermittently, and their attempts to stop are often influenced by changes in circumstances. The factors which influence their chances of stopping are continuing to live at home into their 20s, being successful at school and avoiding the influence of other offenders (friends, partners and siblings), using drugs (particularly hard drugs) and heavy drinking.

Different approaches to preventing crime have been tried over the last 25 years. Policies have been shaped by views about the relative weights to be given to economic and/or emotional deprivation, and individuals' abilities and encouragement to behave responsibly.

A recent Home Office research report recommended a number of broad and far-reaching preventative measure to combat youth crime:

- strengthening families – for example, through family centres and support groups;
- strengthening schools – for example, through strategies to prevent truancy;
- protecting young people (particularly young men) from the influence of delinquents in their peer group and from high risk activities such as alcohol and drug abuse; and
- preparing young people for fully independent and responsible adulthood, associated with social and life skills education and education for citizenship.

Clearly these would have a wide range of impacts on young people beyond the area of crime and delinquency, and would need many years of redirected investment.

Leisure

The most common use of free time by young people is watching TV or listening to the radio, on average 14 hours per week. Outside the home young people commonly go to the cinema or participate in sport. Young people need leisure facilities which will give them a safe environment in which to relax, learn social skills and have access to the support and, on occasion, guidance and direction from a significant adult who is not necessarily in a formal position of authority. They have access to sports, the arts and constructive leisure pursuits which are ways of easing the transition to adulthood. The youth service provides organised leisure activity for young people, though its specific learning potential has probably been under-emphasised.

In 1944 local authorities were given statutory but unspecific responsibility for youth work, but they believe that they have never had the capacity to meet the need because many perceive that central government has been reluctant to clarify their duties or provide adequate resources. Central government for its part regards the delivery and funding of local services, including the youth services, as a matter for each local authority, setting their own budget reflecting their own priorities. The government sets the overall framework for the funding of local authority services nationally through the standard spending assessment (SSA) system. The local authority returns for 1994–95 show that expenditure by local authorities on the youth service rose by 3.32 per cent in cash terms (a 0.47 per cent increase in real terms) to £281.8m compared with 1993–94. Levels of spending by LEAs do of course vary from year to year, reflecting changing priorities, so that while over the period 1990–95 funding by them in real terms has been almost level (+0.7 per cent), some areas can report a closure of some youth facilities (e.g. inner London has experienced recent cuts of 20 per cent). Tension and/or mutual blame between central and local governments is clearly not helpful to the cause of young people.

Many independent and voluntary organisations work in the youth services area, though there are still large numbers of young people who decline to participate or have no access. Nevertheless, some three out of five young people are involved in youth work during their formative years, although participation rates are highest for 11 to 14-year-olds.

There is no doubt that well organised youth provision is in the best interests of an educated, mature society, but because its results are long-term, rarely dramatic and difficult to evaluate it is sometimes difficult to attract the necessary funding. More tempting commercial provision does exist, in leisure centres and discos, but the price is often prohibitive, especially when people are on youth wages or are dependent on their parents. Such provision can be exploitative and lacks the personal support, direction and learning focus which is central to youth work.

Family

Unavoidably, family issues weave throughout this report because, while we demur from any notion of a 'golden age' for families, a strong, stable and sensitive home base is a crucial, even ideal launch pad for young people. The traditional family structure for bringing up children and preparing them for adulthood is undergoing major changes. Many adults and their dependants are suffering in the process, characterised fundamentally by insecure relationships, or, in other words, a social crisis of attachment and implicitly of identity. This is not a helpful backcloth for young people seeking theirs.

Throughout the UK the age of marriage is being deferred, cohabitation is increasingly popular and fewer young people are getting married. Among the general population divorce rates have doubled since 1971 and approaching 40 per cent of marriages are now likely to end in divorce. Lone parents account for 21 per cent of all families with dependent children. Families with dependent children, whether with one or two parents, have experienced a growing level of relative economic disadvantage over the past 25 years. It is no longer pensioners who make up the majority in the lowest income bracket, but families with children. There has been a greater spatial concentration of poverty into particular localities – most often inner-city or peripheral housing estates which have populations younger and poorer than the rest of the country. Aside from that there is, for many young people, a poverty of time in interaction with committed adults.

Young people's experience of family life has important effects on their own confidence and attitudes to family life. Yet a range of public policies and commercial practices have tended to promote the individuation rather than the cohesion of households. Many specialists in family policy have argued for a wide range of corrective measures, including much more flexible approaches to work patterns, and a greater emphasis on preparation for partnering and education in parenthood and childcare, extending into the adolescent phase.

When the family ceases to be a unit for protection and becomes a source of danger in young people's lives, the local authority has a legal obligation to look after them. This can either be through a care order or by providing accommodation. The trend in recent years has been to try to provide foster homes for young people rather than to have them adopted or placed in residential care. Over fifty thousand young people are being looked after by local authorities. Their educational attainment tends to be weak, and they later form a very disproportionate element of homeless and prison populations. All too few seem to acquire the inner resilience to thrive despite their disadvantaged circumstances.

In Summary

In this brief review it seems to us that the overall balance sheet for young people suggests that the 'terms of trade' have moved sharply against them over the past 20 years. In terms of direct and indirect transfers between generations there have been reductions in psychosocial security, personalised time investment, wages, benefits, grants and allowances. Many of the services that provide directly for the young have not increased their share of resources.

Responsive services, such as youth provision have, at best, had broadly level funding amid rising needs, alongside a growth in provision often designed to control and contain the young. Young people's positive achievements (more qualifications, longer time in education and training) are often taken for granted, while the media tend to focus on young people's negativity.

The young have borne too much of the cost of structural change in both the economy and social norms about home stability and caring. Their transitions to adult life have become extended and problematic, as the next chapter briefly examines.

But young people are not homogenous and there is some evidence of widening gaps between the successful and unsuccessful – in education, qualifications, jobs, health and recorded crime – evident in some ethnic minority groups and in specific localities. Some have become disconnected from the democratic process, neither voting nor registering to do so. Many, including now some young graduates with understandable expectations, feel surplus to requirements, yet most of these will all too soon parent the next generation. A decent society cannot function in the modern era by even unintended processes which imply that exclusion, and the creation of a permanent or semi-permanent 'underclass' early in life, is even reluctantly acceptable.

Chapter 3

Youth transitions to adult life

THE PRIME overall social, psychological and practical task of youth is the transition to adult life. This confers greater independence and incorporates changes in roles and responsibilities. While in important ways the function of infant and childhood growth is preparation for adulthood, the adolescent/youth phase involves much more explicit and targeted 'personal work' – for that is what it is – towards the demands of independence as a young adult.

Acquiring adult *status* is of central importance to becoming an adult. This process of status acquisition is complex, and is socially and culturally defined. There are four particular areas where adulthood is achieved:

- employment and the wage which goes with it;
- independent living;
- independent relationships, parenting and parenthood; and
- independence as a consumer in the marketplace.

These forms of adult status differ by expectations associated with class and by gender, while achieving adulthood status is not necessarily experienced simplistically. Parenthood may precede marriage or young people may return for periods to live with parents after leaving home. In practice not all young people follow mapped out stages, some are missed out and others reversed.

Historically, young people's citizenship has been experienced as a series of transitions which are cited within areas such as the movement from school to work or going to university. These transitions still remain central, but changes in social policy and the moral economy have influenced how young people experience these transitions and therefore their citizenship. Having a vote at the age of 18, as a symbol of political participation is for many young people 'no big deal' compared with other symbols of status.

Symbolically, for most, the key move towards adult status focuses upon the process of leaving home, or of leaving care for those young people who are not fortunate to have a place shared with others which they can truly call 'home'.

There is widespread agreement that leaving home is now best seen in our kind of society as a process over time rather than as a single event. Indeed, it is rare for fleeing the human nest to be a sudden and conclusive event. Hence, in terms of personal development, the great majority of youth tasks, in transition to adulthood, crystallise upon the demands of leaving home safely.

Among the *tasks of leaving home safely* are:

- securing a place to live, and 'a job' (which may initially be full-time study with perhaps some casual employment or structured volunteering in the college vacations);
- establishing a healthy lifestyle with sufficient routine and a balanced diet;
- sound money and time management, including leisure pursuits;
- establishing and maintaining friendships and social support;
- dealing with intimacy, emotions and personal sexuality, including the options of partnering and parenthood; and
- acquiring skills and experience to service all these goals and related transition tasks, so that poor choices or 'blind mistakes' may be minimised.

We believe that these objectives have become more demanding within contemporary society. They are also grossly underrated within the learning priorities of our educational system, as explicit targets within the youth service and in youth work more widely. Quite normally the process of transition involves tugs between dependence and individualism, and there is generally an ambivalence for both young people and parents as 'standing on your own feet' vies with 'letting go'.

Within the leaving home tasks outlined inevitably lies the complex process of establishing a sufficient personal and social identity. If this is not reasonably achieved in its fundamentals at this stage of life, a range of personal and societal disadvantages with high economic costs are likely to arise later on in the life-cycle. Hence the transition of youth to adulthood, including the leaving home aspect, is of crucial significance for public policy. It is never a purely private nor circumscribed matter.

The foregoing task list (page 32) involves both opportunity and resources for targeted personal development activities, for research and common observation show that the leaving home process is far more diverse than it was even 20 years ago. Apart from action knowledge and skills, a psychological readiness to separate safely from parents or parent figures is involved. Psychodynamically the leaving home process is the next most important separation to the event of birthing. Safe separation at this stages presumes that prior experiences of parental-type attachments have on balance been rewarding.

We cannot here elaborate the crucial issue of sound parent-child attachment in earlier phases, except to note that early and developing security (but not claustrophobia) from such attachments greatly helps the older young person to separate safely from home when the time comes. It is a matter of grave importance for future youth and society that a range of pressures are markedly undermining the strength of crucial early and later parent-child bonds in a very significant proportion of families. Sufficient consistency and warmth in caregiving from a small number of parent figures is a vital ingredient in human welfare.

Without specific educational and therapeutic interventions, which could and must involve activities within mainstream youth work, the transmission of insecure attachment from one generation to another is worryingly high. Preparation of youth for the options of partnering and parenting thus needs to be a very high priority in our view.

A Scottish study has, for example, shown that one in three youth home departures were measurably problematic, with absent or periodic fathers often being an associated factor. Many leaving home transitions are sadly unplanned responses to domestic and familial crisis. When this happens young people can readily become locked into a downward spiral, including homelessness and the multiple risks from 'bad company' subcultures.

Elements of predictability, some continuity and threads in a personal script assist in transitional safety. Transitions become more difficult where everything changes fairly swiftly and little is carried through from the past. Strategy, tactics and not excessive practical and time pressure, together with relevant educational preparation, are ingredients for successful leaving home transitions.

Family of origin circumstances and dynamics tend to be highly significant in terms of outcomes. Parental insight and patience are often required. Hence youth policy cannot be detached from public policy factors which affect family well-being more widely. Implicitly, however, we believe that the tasked focus provided by the leaving home process is a rich seam for practical educational objectives within youth work, capable of much greater creative and stimulating mediation to all young people.

Chapter 4

Voices of and for youth: the need to listen

OUR WORK HAS been time-limited and therefore our scope to engage in new empirical research has been very restricted, and properly so because our experience and reading of the literature suggested strongly that there was sufficient known already upon which to advance practical policies which are more youth-friendly.

Nonetheless we have sampled fresh youth opinion and that of appropriate officers of agencies working for young people. In the former case, small groups of young people from a number of local youth councils in England and Scotland attended a 24-hour residential event at St George's House, Windsor, at the end of May 1996. For the professional officers, a postal questionnaire was circulated during that month.

Views of Young People

The residential event programme was organised by the British Youth Council, and young people were briefed about the remit of the Working Group and informed that they were being consulted about youth policy in an open-ended manner. For most of the time they worked in two groups, each with a facilitator and an observing member of the Working Group. Group findings were reported in a concluding plenary session.

Trouble was taken with this exercise because we believe that understanding young people's opinions, aspirations and reasonable expectations is fundamental to building a workable, effective youth policy. The British Youth Council also drew to our attention a range of recent survey findings about young people's views about jobs, politics, crime, social and moral attitudes, and education and training.

Although the soundings of young people taken at Windsor inevitably covered but a small sample, the process was one of consultation in some depth and produced some important insights which served to corroborate much other advocacy. The results of this exercise are now presented.

Our sample groups of young people in residence brainstormed issues and concerns as perceived by them. The summaries of their output are shown in Table 2, largely in their own words. It will be noted that there is a range of similarities between the two group summaries.

Table 2:
Young people's concerns; Group summaries

Group A	Group B
1 Distrust of the political system. Little respect for local and national politicians, perceived too often as self-seeking and play acting.	1 Young people do not have a voice that can be properly heard, and experience improper discrimination based upon distorted stereotypes.
2 Need for political education, including the working of government and the legal system. Also needed is practical experience of genuinely delegated civic responsibility.	2 Cynicism about the value of voting, and tokenism among adults over youth participation in civic life.
3 Need for specific focus on and resources for the leaving home process, in which adequate accommodation for independent living is crucial.	3 Youth training system needs more status and quality, and based upon proper consultation with young people.

4   Schooling should include more personal and social development topics with status, such as health, emotions and relationships, citizenship and the law, using team approaches with other agencies, especially for medical aspects. Stronger peer education would avoid patronising approaches.

5   Health service is often intimidating for young people. Approaches to health, including sex education, are not taught in relation to human emotions.

6   Media misrepresent young people and omit to give good news about them. Hard for us to overcome unfair images, especially in the job market.

7   Inadequate information provision concerning youth opportunities (doubts about the Careers Service). Lack of jobs and recognition of voluntary work by prospective employers.

8   The teaching of history is often biased and too ethnocentric, making it unhelpful to contemporary social relations.

4   Social and community education should be a part of the core curriculum. Need to build up young people's confidence and social and financial skills. Education must become more relevant.

5   Youth services under-resourced, and would be more attractive if peer led. Problem of youth club images. Youth workers need re-educating as catalysts not controllers.

6   Relative unfairness in being dealt with by the police and legal system – for example, presuming that young people are at the heart of protests.

7   Lack of job opportunities and persistent catch 22 cycle of no experience, no job, no experience. Use of young people as cheap labour without power.

8   Inconsistent age discrimination criteria with respect to a range of adult functions, that is, when the law allows young people to do what.

We now quote some memorable statements within groups' feedback:

- *No political party has serious. long-term policies for young people. Those in power are out of touch with much of today's reality for young people.*
- *Look at the mess the country is in partly because young people are not being listened to. We are the voice for tomorrow and society is moving very fast.*
- *Generally we are undervalued and seen as an economic and social burden, too often being scapegoats for not giving to our communities.*
- *Young people are not apathetic and don't want an easy life – so much of society's attitude to us is based upon false assumptions, because of things like appearance and musical and social tastes.*
- *We need to challenge our elders' attitudes towards our desire for real participation as young citizens.*
- *We get a lot of mutual respect from peer conformity in contrast to the lack of respect we feel from adults – you can be OK even if you are not white, have a tattoo and don't wear a suit.*
- *Young people tend to behave as a consequence of the way they are treated, just like anyone else. We respect those whose respect we feel.*
- *Why should we wish to conform within a society which doesn't really value its people?*
- *NVQ means not very qualified.*
- *Young people are easily intimidated by adults. We dislike being patronised and are not automatically deferential because of someone's age. I don't trust adults more than my own age group.*
- *We have really valued being consulted for your report. It is unusual for us to be admitted to decision-making processes which affect our lives.*

We observe that these young people come from quite 'ordinary' backgrounds, but because they were on local youth councils, they spoke with a mandate. None of their demands seemed to us to be unreasonable. With regard to employment they were not demanding jobs, just better preparation in order to take up what market forces are generating. They do not regard their situation as hopeless in the face of substantial unemployment, but feel let down by a lack of suitable preparation, wanting to be better equipped to join in.

To a degree these young people saw themselves and many of their peers as victims of mobility and social disintegration, and regretted the lack of family stability. Now that the transition from school to work was much longer, they often fell into what they saw as a void between the two.

Leaving home was seen by them as a crucial step in the transition to adulthood, but for many was becoming an increasingly difficult process. The lack of cheap rented accommodation was an immediate problem which with low benefit rates and lack of work opportunities means that many young people cannot cope financially living independently. Assistance in learning how to manage the little money at their disposal was considered valuable, but had not been provided at school, as if school was merely a preparation for further dependence. The role played by the families of young people was perceived as crucial to the success that moving away from the family home can be. Family support in the first years of independent living was considered vital since the state provides very little.

Concerning youth services, a lack of provision was emphasised, particularly for 14 to 18-year-olds – the 'gap' between many youth clubs' cut-off and night club eligibility. But it was seen as essential that participative governance be initiated. By way of example it was noted that the St Helens youth clubs are run by a members committee to whom the manager is accountable. If the committee was dissatisfied it could go to the principal youth officer or to the youth council who had access to the local council. They have real power, including the power to sack poor managers. Moreover the youth council members had had training in participation and committee skills in a series of residential weekends. They visited Brussels and Strasbourg and met with MEPs and MPs. They maintained that if you trust people they will respond positively.

The overriding message of these soundings was that due to structural factors out of their control, particularly in family, neighbourhood and employment, today's young people need to be treated differently to those in the past. For most, their circumstances had changed significantly and the adult world had for the most part been both somewhat indifferent and slow to respond. Many social indicators pointed to the need now for urgent policy responses.

Yet we met a combination of cynicism and indifference about

political processes, as has been reflected in a number of far better sampled studies of young people's attitudes to political allegiance and participation. Young people express concern about politicians and believe that too often they are doing a poor job of setting and upholding moral standards. While this is no doubt also the view of many adults, a cynicism among the young about the practice of so-called democratic processes, whether through lack of understanding of the complexities of the public square or disillusionment with the motives and actions of public officers, is we believe serious. Our investment in and concern for young people are necessary components countering the cynicism, alienation and low self-esteem which is felt among too many. Moreover this is seen to be a matter for all political parties rather than a crude indictment of recent governments.

Responses from youth organisations

As noted, the Working Group compiled a deliberately short questionnaire (see Appendix A, page 81) circulated to some 70 youth-related organisations of whom about half replied (see Appendix B, page 83) through appropriate officers within the timescale; no reminders were sent. The purpose of this exercise was to take soundings largely from those responsible for a range of fieldwork services for young people on a handful of dimensions:

a) core principles to undergird youth policy – see Chapter 5, page 47;
b) strengths and weaknesses of current youth policies;
c) strengths of and constraints on agencies' work;
d) agencies' main anxieties about today's youth; and
e) policy developments which agencies see as urgent.

Replies reflected both voluntary sector and local government interests with the former predominating, appropriately we felt since it probably reflects a greater diversity of both provision and community concern and goodwill beyond the ballot box. There was much maturity and realism in replies and we now distil the balance of responses to dimensions (b) to (e) as listed above.

Strengths and weaknesses of policy and practice

Although the form of the questionnaire within the areas (a) to (e) above was deliberately open-ended (we did not provide substantive trigger words) almost half of respondents specifically referred both to (i) incoherence and inconsistency, and (ii) inadequate investment, as *weaknesses* of current youth policy. Other terms echoed some of what we had heard from young people, for example:

- youth is a low priority, leaders are out of touch with young people and there is no clear legal mandate for the youth service;
- responses tend to be short-term and distorted by over-complex funding regimes;
- youth work falls under at least five departments of central Government with no properly funded lead department to deal with it;
- inadequate training of youth workers within confused ideologies of purpose; and
- poor dissemination of good practice.

Strengths within such policies as are in place were seen to include:

- strong NGO commitment with rewarding partnerships with statutory sector;
- opportunity for innovation and greater sensitivity towards individuals in some fieldwork; and
- some very dedicated workers, including those from disciplines other than youth work.

There were, however, far fewer mentions of strengths. One notable agency in the environmental field, which has been able to tap into young people's ' single issue' political concern for that area, noted that apart from the Department for Education and Employment's valuable, if limited, scheme of grant aid for national voluntary youth organisations 'we struggled to find strengths in current youth policies'.

A key overall strategic theme is reflected in the following quotations from major players in the youth scene:

- *The tendency persists of viewing young people as citizens of the future as opposed to stakeholders of the present ... young people are underrated within society.*

> • *There is a lack of generational accounting for young people. The lessons from the USA about the long-term impact of powerful grey lobbies are chilling. We must achieve a broad view of how spending on young people compares with that for the rest of the community ... (by taking) ... a holistic view of their needs.*

Agencies' main anxieties about young people

The most frequent specific mentions here (from about a third of respondents) were:

- increasing marginalisation, exclusion and disaffection (affecting perhaps 30 per cent of young people); and
- lack of appropriate education, training and employment opportunities.

However, other categories of response often related to these two broad headings and/or overlapped issues raised by our sample of young people, with the lack of education appropriate to future lives, including the option of parenthood, being highlighted. One agency referred specifically to the 'inability of the state machinery to deal with the educational deprivation of young parents, especially young mothers'. Other anxieties worthy of note were expressed as:

- emotional health and personal identity at risk;
- lack of initiation into values other than materialism;
- detachment from the natural world and ideas of sustainability;
- lack of reliable opportunities for social mixing;
- television and video violence regularly portrayed in improper contexts;
- depopulation of young people from rural areas; and
- too much competitive pressure and harsh distinctions between winners and losers.

Policy developments seen as urgent

Consistent with the above, coherent initiatives in relevant education and training were mentioned by 40 per cent of respondents, while youth employment and youth service funding were each raised in a quarter of replies. Other mentions, including family support, again overlapped with the concerns expressed by young people. One agency wished 'each relevant Government department to be challenged to come up with preventative programmes, including enabling better early parenting skills, more training in enterprise as microdemocracy', with the Treasury being convinced of the necessity of major funding, and well organised research and development. This does not demand a 'big government' response; rather government acting as a facilitator of others' energies and activities within a proper framework of accountability.

In summary, what emerges from these soundings is a broad consistency of policy concern from young people and the agencies, both voluntary (including churches) and statutory, which seek to serve them. Underpinning these and sometimes explicitly expressed, are concerns about personal values (materialism and relativism), social ethics and justice, family breakdown and the need for the adult population to see young people as 'architects of a new social vision' and not largely as 'problems'.

The overall picture is thus not one prompting any complacency. Furthermore, within our soundings we were satisfied that the more obvious markers of special pleading and vested interests were not the drivers of views expressed. Indeed, we have the impression of high field commitment with, as one respondent put it, 'many professional youth workers operating in situations where young people are under great stress and finding life difficult'. Yet this commitment, when present, is clearly set within a confused and often irritating policy situation, in which skilled time and energy, which should be showered on and with young people, is distracted by administrative-related survival or worse.

Chapter 5

Core principles for youth policy

THIS CHAPTER draws upon the two consultations at St George's House, Windsor Castle referred to in Chapter 1, and also substantially upon the first part of the Working Group's questionnaire which was sent to representative organisations and institutions and referred to in the second part of Chapter 4.

The Working Group noted as significant the issues and themes which have consistently emerged throughout both consultations and in the responses to the questionnaire. These in our view must be taken seriously, as they provide considerable validity and credibility to our later proposals. We believe that these proposals draw upon what many experienced professionals working with young people, and a wide diversity of national youth organisations providing services for young people, both experience and perceive as the state of current youth policy and the need for a new youth policy in Britain today. Within this we believed it was important, not least for non-specialists, to clarify core principles within the case for policy renewal and for the improvement of practice within schemes and services for youth.

All public policy is set within macro sociological, cultural, ethical, political and economic perceptions. These are fluid and can be modified so as to affect forms of social control, scope of choices, and personal, sectional and collective opportunities.

In previous chapters we have referred to several criticisms of current youth policies. The main one is that they are individually set within a very partial vision, with no reference to an overall framework. A more rational and indeed efficient youth policy would be based upon a set of national core principles and values, which would themselves convey to young people the value placed on them as stakeholders. These would recognise their need to experience an effective transition to adulthood and full citizenship, and which confirms society's commitment to their complete well-being.

Such principles would, for example, include the importance of encouraging the personal assumption of responsibility by young people, their right to appropriate consultation, participation and influence, their right to protection from all forms of exploitation, their entitlement to grow up in a safe and healthy environment, the entitlement to raise their educational, vocational, social and employment potential and opportunities, and to be able to form in due course their own collaborative households and families.

But this language of rights and entitlements, however justified, is empty without adults' willingness to take appropriate responsibility, including powers of delegation, and make appropriate investments, involving some other sectional sacrifices in order that they might be generally delivered. We are under no illusion that policies to support youth transitions will be hard to achieve, even if there is sufficient political will. It is imperative that a long-term view is taken based upon a fundamental secure valuing of young people. Yet a long-term view will mean little beyond what one of our informants termed 'glittering generalities' if such is not marked by the launch and implementation of new national and local plans.

We believe that the very presence of a written national youth policy, which some other countries have, would in itself go some way to conveying to young people their value and worth. There has to be as an aspect of such a policy a better understanding of the problems which society poses for young people, rather than largely fixing our gaze the other way round.

This is first a humanitarian rather than party political matter. Indeed the broad principles of youth policy, necessarily long-term issues, must be capable of important continuities between Parliaments. This stricture applies to much other social policy if it is to be effective and sound investment of the taxed and voluntary contributions of the whole society. The Joint Approach to Social Policy (JASP) advocated by the 10 Downing Street Policy Unit over 20 years ago has scarcely been heeded and at great cost to the social ecology.

Key words in the design of youth policies should include **protection**, **participation**, **potential**, and **provision** (of effective structures for providers). It is suggested that these words themselves imply a set of values about how policies should be shaped, while the cost of an effective youth policy should take account of the costs we incur in not having one.

The core principles for a youth policy which have emerged at both the St George's House consultations and in the questionnaire replies have an encouraging consistency and can be reasonably simply expressed. Moreover, they are strongly suggestive in terms of action – both of content and methods.

The core principles which it was felt should underpin youth policy identified in response to the open, not triggered, response questionnaire were in order of highest percentage responses:

1 Equality of esteem and opportunity (40 per cent)
2 Empowerment of young people (33 per cent)
3= Participation by and of young people (30 per cent)
3= Preparation and development of young people socially and personally (30 per cent)
4= Coherence – the need for policies to be research-informed and inter-related to provide consistency and efficiency (20 per cent)
4= Challenge for young people (20 per cent)

With 'the equality of esteem' aspect, the concern is to express within a universal framework that all young people, being of equal worth, should have access to relevant assistance in their transition to adulthood, and that this should be sensitive to individual need. Implied is the associated need to communicate sincerely to young people their value and worth though practical programmes and projects with proper investment and a broader vision of educational accounting.

With regard to the empowerment aspect we see this as being largely through the serious preparation of all young people for adulthood and citizenship and the particular responsibilities which go with it.

Reviewing our sources within the value-laden key words mentioned previously, viz:

protection – reflecting that young people are vulnerable and need boundaries appropriate to their development

participation – there is no lasting learning without active engagement

potential – to be skilfully identified and drawn out

provision – structures and mechanisms for service to the young

... we feel able to articulate the following *core principles*:

A national youth policy should promote *six core objectives*:

1 **Responsible empowerment** – mainly through much greater emphasis upon well-structured educational preparation for adulthood, with associated lifeskills, well informed by research-based information and concepts.

2 **Sustainable, equitable programmes** which give every young person patient opportunity to find themselves and develop their potential.

3 **Clear inter-relation between relevant disciplines** – education, employment, personal finance, health and environment.

4 **Keen awareness of human inter-dependencies** in family, community, nationally and globally.

5 **Youth participation** through imaginative activities which tap hidden motivations, provide for fun as well as reflection, and both confer and enhance individual dignity.

6 **Proper consultation** between all stakeholders – government, scheme and service providers, and young people themselves.

These six target areas of both substance and style will remain vacuous good intentions without three core conditions:

1 a thorough long-term strategy;

2 a tighter statutory framework within which youth providers operate; and

3 a major shift of resources within those allocated to young people already and incrementally from other areas of the economy.

These conditions are interconnected. Too many young people are not connected, or belonging, and there are creative savings to be made long-term if only we can draw them in from the 'virtual communities' which many of them inhabit. Disaffection and alienation are reversible, but not through hands which are either disrespectful or mean. As one respondent put it:

> *'Young people's lives are currently more complex than ever before, yet less support than ever is available.'*

So the means have to be willed, and unswervingly, by the voting population, including of course grandparents who are an important aspect of the needed intergenerational 'compact'.

We next move on to considering the core principles of a youth policy in terms of a policy map which can facilitate their delivery. In this we are undaunted by a problematic history going back to aspects of the 1944 Butler Act, The 1960 Albemarle Report and the Thompson Report of 1982.

Chapter 6

Towards a map for youth policy: content and proposals

H ISTORICALLY, the development of such policies as there have been towards young people have been guided by two principles – their protection, and enabling them to fulfil their potential. Young people are naturally drawn towards three goals – useful work with appropriate economic underpinning, living independently with or without others, and participative citizenship.

Social changes prompt regular reviews for each generation of the steps needed to achieve these goals. Thus, for instance, the appropriate questioning of the extent to which contemporary education and training systems are attuned to equipping all young people for adult and working life.

In this chapter, we endeavour to outline a substantive and procedural map for youth policy. Such a map we believe is necessary if central and local government, voluntary organisations, parents, young people and communities more widely are to work collectively and efficiently towards much improved outcomes for youth.

In terms of input towards this mapping task we have analysed the national youth policy documents of five other countries, other reports on youth policy (including youth services) produced within our own country over the past few years, and reflected upon various options for the generic grouping of youth concerns. Our goal was to achieve substantive validity for youth agenda while achieving sufficient simplicity of focus to enable policy. In addition, we have endeavoured to use the creative thinking concerning this aspect which was carried out within the group work of the November 1995 St George's House consultation. That included work not only on youth policy principles (now incorporated here within Chapter 5), but also on youth 'entitlements' within a Young Person's Charter (see Appendix C, page 85), mechanisms for policy delivery (in which genuine collaborative partnerships were seen as essential) and on accountability connections between key players.

Content analysis

Content analysis of the national youth policy documents of Sweden, Malta, Finland, Germany and Israel enabled a wide variety of topics to be grouped provisionally under eight headings:

Generic Grouping of Youth Issues

1 **Youth Employment Issues**
   Working conditions for young people/voluntary service and compulsory non-military service/community service/Youth Enterprise/improved special, remedial, vocational training.

2 **Youth Organisations and Support Structures**
   Support to voluntary and other youth organisations/Directory of Youth Organisations/National Youth Centre/youth worker training.

3 **Education**
   Driving attitudes and values/youth idealism/young families and parenthood/duties of young people.

4 **Influence for Young People**
   Youth councils/national youth forums/representation on government committees/young people as a positive force for change.

5 **International Dimension**
   Youth exchanges/youth mobility/bilateral agreements/special international relations.

6 **Law/Protection**
   UN Convention on Children's Rights/threshold age limits/drugs, mental and physical health issues/bullying/law on adoption.

7 **Provisions**
   Culture and young people/youth information/young people and the environment/national Youth Day/Youth Card/special housing

provision for young people/young people in sport, the arts and national youth facilities/franchising (e.g. The Duke of Edinburgh's Award).

8 **Targeted Support**

Special needs/young people at risk (e.g. homelessness)/action research on youth issues/work reflecting appropriate gender differentiation/actions to combat racism and xenophobia/crime prevention and work against violence/intergenerational contact and community initiatives/actions to support minorities.

We noted that these topics also mirror youth agenda and concerns in the UK.

Regrouping these with a degree of internal logic, and in a manner which reflects something of our categories of key recommendations in Chapter 7, we suggest the following focusses for the content of youth policies, each to be superimposed upon the values and principles outlined in Chapter 5.

Content focusses for youth policy

A Civic influence for young people.

B Employment issues.

C Education for adulthood and responsible citizenship through schools and community provision, including:
- targeted support for distinctive needs; and
- help for parents of teenagers and young adults.

D Youth organisations, structures and collaboration, including:
- youth services; and
- international dimension and exchange.

E Issues of law and protection.

As we have noted, a coherent youth policy will embrace key areas affecting young people's lives. We recognise that there are a number of players responsible for ensuring that these areas are covered – for example, the family, the community, the State and of course the young people themselves.

The youth policy would state that all young people may expect from society the essentials of food, clothing and shelter, which may be expressed in terms of a stable income, housing, education and training, protection from violence and ill-health, employment or a gainful use of their time, the development of themselves as citizens and as whole persons, and access to the level of power in matters that affect them directly.

The policy would seek to rationalise and humanise the many thresholds to adulthood through a holistic examination of the transition from childhood and dependency. But while these thresholds may always require a chronological age element, there would be a recognition that, given the diversity of the developmental needs of young people, age limits sometimes need flexible interpretation.

Responsibility for safeguarding the legitimate key expectations of young people requires transitions from family caring, working in collaboration with state provisions, through the individual. Every young person has an evolving life trajectory so that it is not appropriate to define, and certainly not to fix, the point at which responsibility passes from one 'provider' to the other in each field. But in accord with the principle of inclusion (Chapter 5) there has to be a minimum expectation, as of right, for all young people. While the state must not seek to be the main provider, it has a duty to provide when all else fails. A key factor in the success of policy would be to make the roles of provider and guarantor clear.

The task of achieving a coherent youth policy is not impossibly daunting. Much of the 'furniture' is in existence, through legislation or provision managed by different sectors of national and local government, but often it is in the wrong place or not linked together. A youth policy maps what is being done or not done, to meet the needs of young people. It aims to improve the cooperation between agencies which address the several aspects of young people's lives.

A coherent youth policy does not imply a single set of legislation or a monolithic agency with exclusive competence for all matters affecting young people. It aims to question the compartmentalisation of functions whose separation can work against the interests of those it seeks to help. But before examining youth policy machinery, we briefly look at the five content focusses above.

Our proposals

A.   The first tenet of a youth policy is to give **greater civic influence** to the young. In part this is already happening through co-opting young people onto consultative groups. The Government supports the British Youth Council to represent the views of young people and promote their greater empowerment, while more locally, properly constituted youth councils debate and sometimes have executive powers concerning some factors which affect young people's lives.

Putting a young person onto bodies that exercise power can be unsatisfactory. Not only are these a minority presence, but co-members are often professionals whose working lives are bound up with the issues in hand. The young people are often not up to speed on the matters discussed, poorly briefed and without the skills or experience to be effective. Their inputs are discounted, their interest waivers and their membership lapses. Their disinterest becomes a self-fulfilling prophecy.

Perhaps the most effective way to consult young people is through youth councils where the young people are in the majority. They tackle issues at their own pace, have a common appreciation of the issues and are freer to express their views. Youth councils can act as a 'second chamber' to youth-proof local legislation. Youth Councils need briefing and they need a channel for their views to be taken into account by local politicians. We have seen evidence of youth councils operating to good effect.

Young people should be consulted on matters that affect them at national level through a body made up of representatives from local youth councils. There should be a formal channel for their considered views to be heard by government. In some other countries the national parliament building is given over to a young people's parliament during the recess, attracting attention from the press.

There is the risk that young people will make uncomfortable or extravagant demands. It is our view that they are no more or less likely to do so than adults; their decisions will be constrained by the same practicalities and their powers would only be advisory. Youth councils will bring young people into the political process, allow priorities to be drawn based on their experience and admit their ideas and their vitality.

We go further and say that in areas targeted specially at the young, like the youth service, young people should have substantial representation on management committees, with officers accountable to them. At a national level we have seen evidence of national youth councils being given status on mixed commissions for the implementation of national policies.

B. Regarding **employment**, much of significance has already been noted. Securing long-term paid employment is a landmark in achieving full adult status. An income changes the relation of dependency that characterises childhood. Government has been right to place emphasis on the attainment of employment. Equipping then enabling young people to get a job is the first priority of youth policy, and there need to be many stepping stones which will bridge the capricious nature of employment market forces, low self-image and motivation, and relevant up-skilling.

After leaving school there are three basic routes a young person can follow between the ages of 16 to 18: get a job, join a YT scheme, or remain in full-time education studying now for a wider range of qualifications than was the case even a decade ago. Current policy states that all young people shall be accommodated in one of these three categories. For the majority it is satisfactory. It implicitly extends governmental responsibility for young people to 18. But there is a fall out from all three streams and particularly from YT.

We believe that there should be provision for all young people to the age of 18 after leaving school. It should offer five options:

1 further full-time education;
2 full-time employment with some employer guarantee of skill-enhancing training;
3 Youth Training leading to vocational qualifications;
4 supervised and well-structured Civic Service Work (CSW); and
5 youth-driven learning within clear objectives.

The first three of these options are already in place. There is a need for wider options or a mix of them to cater for those falling through the net of what should be a comprehensive policy. Reaching the most disadvantaged needs flexible yet secure options.

Civic Service Work on a full-time or part-time basis should be available to all young people up to the age of 25 who wish to do it. We hope that it would also become attractive to young people from any of the three current schemes, and if properly managed and presented it may offer opportunity to those for whom the current options are seen as too limited. CSW could offer constructive engagement without necessarily demanding paper qualifications. It could motivate young people to seek a course of training, or help them to secure full-time employment in sectors that draw on the skills and experience they learned directly or as a by-product of CSW. We would presume that existing funded schemes of volunteering would form part of overall CSW, in which 'W' stands for real work with real economic value. A recent Henley Centre/Mori poll of young people showed that no less than two-thirds would be willing to participate in (an undefined form of) Civic Service. Hence, well thought out, with monitored pilot schemes and effective marketing, we believe that CSW would prove popular.

In youth-driven learning schemes young people are given grants, either singly or in groups, to undertake a project of their own choosing. Current models having their successes are The Prince's Trust and the Youth Initiatives aspect of the Youth for Europe programme. The young people that drop out of the FE and YT sectors often do so consciously, not because they lack the ability to follow the courses set. They have ability but cannot channel it along directed paths. Allowing them to develop projects of their own harnessed motivation can liberate entrepreneurial skills that help them to solve their own problems. This is learning that can be built upon by measured training input and lead to qualifications. It can also lead young people to have the confidence to start up their own businesses.

These five options, which can be blended, are not exhaustive. All bodies dealing with young people should be searching for constructive activities that will engage 16 to 18-year-olds and thereby enhance their learning, skills and experience and equip them for the labour market. A greater number of options will attract a greater percentage of the cohort and reduce drop-out.

On completion of this multioption scheme, young people who still have no job or a course in full-time education continue to be a charge to the social security budget. A comprehensive youth policy requires a second level of employment enhancement programmes by commuting benefits to subsidise them. A programme for 18 to 21-year-olds and then as required for 21 to 25-year-olds would build on its precursor's offering, for example, community service in another member state of the European Union. Another option is work placement schemes giving extended work placements, or grants to establish small businesses, and surrogate social programmes run by the young people themselves under arms-length supervision and tutelage of professional agencies. By the age of 18 the number of young people without either places in HE or gainful employment is small. Higher rung programmes represent a continuation of the active management of young people's potential, with essentially a three-tiered safety net.

We believe that there should be targeted activities for special at risk young people. In schools, children with special education needs are identified individually and targeted for special educational help. The same provision does not exist for young people who opt out of all systems and become homeless, or suffer repeated exclusions from school, or fail to register under programmes of training, community service and so on.

Our youth policy requires the deliberate targeting of these young people by school attendance officers, the police, probation service and outreach youth workers. They would identify those who are not enrolled, approach them to follow a diagnostic programme and evaluate how they might best be offered opportunities from which they benefit, such as personal tutoring, special training, remedial training or adventure programmes. The greater diversity of options at 16 to 18 will reduce this problem and increase the range of alternatives open to engage them.

Systematic tackling of this issue would need liaison mechanisms between the various bodies involved, referral and diagnostic procedures, implementation procedures and the widespread use of expenses paid adult volunteers to offer input to the controlled learning of these special cases. Many of the most vulnerable young people have little access to long-term human support; a critical friend or adviser attached to them for months rather than weeks, as pioneered by The Prince's Trust, forms part of the solution to disadvantage. The Working Group would see an enhanced role for the youth service in this targeted work, building on the experience of projects in the Youth Action scheme. We believe that by targeting those who are most excluded there will be concomitant reduction in petty crime and its on-costs.

C.   In relation to **education**, all children and young people should attend school from the age of 5 to 16. This is an aspect of youth policy, although its implementation is the responsibility of the formal education sector. However, at the upper end of the compulsory schooling system the youth policy has a number of stipulations, including consultation about programmes of ' study. Young people have views about their preparation for post-school life, both in terms of the practicalities of everyday living and concerning important questions of relationships and the skills of parenthood.

A comprehensive research-informed syllabus of personal and social education should we believe be drawn up to teach young people about values, rights and duties, to give them unbiased political education, to encourage self-understanding and effective time and money management for independent living, and teach relational skills needed to deal with young families and parenthood. Such learning, which was traditionally taught in the home and community for a far less complex world, is suffering as a consequence of family fragmentation, and other curricular demands often perceived rather short-sightedly as more important. The responsibility for teaching may be divided between the schools and other institutions such as the churches or the youth service. The delivery of activity-related instruction need not rest solely with teachers but could be carefully supplemented by community leaders, some parents, local civil servants and other professionals. However, there should be a policy in place in every area that guarantees all young people a codified exposure to the syllabus content.

A comprehensive youth policy will not allow children to truant extensively nor to be excluded from a succession of schools, suggesting the need for early preventative investment.

There are a number of educationally relevant provisions for young people available through government agencies, the private sector and NGOs. These are often made as part of a more general offering to the population at large. Within each of these activities there should be a defined access to young people so that they become an extension of the opportunities required through the rest of the youth policy.

Local arts and sports councils and other cultural institutions, such as public libraries, should actively involve young people as both participants and consumers. Environmental groups and organisations giving access to the countryside and the national heritage should involve young people as consumers and members both openly and in collaboration with youth organisations such as the Youth Hostel Association and Brathay Hall. Outdoor activity centres and recreation facilities should involve young people more fully in their management and operation. Within all these options there is scope for major extension of the Youth Card scheme.

Also educationally-related are the mass media and youth information. The media and broadcasting agencies should operate more closely in collaboration with young people, both in the formulation of policy and in the provision of content of those sectors that address young people in particular.

There should be a revitalisation of youth information. There is generous public provision nationally and through local government of information delivery systems, and also help from Citizen's Advice Bureaux. The Careers Service is targeted at young people. However, there could be far more customising of agency offerings for young people. We believe that there should be a comprehensive review of information and advice provision in order to make better use of available resources.

D. Concerning **international dimensions** young people should be well informed about other countries and have opportunities to grow to understand North/South issues through the Development Education Association and agencies working in the charity sector. They should have the opportunity to contact, travel to and host their contemporaries in other countries important to the UK through bilateral relations, underpinned by agreements and assistance to undertake youth exchanges and other mobility initiatives. There should also be support for a full participation in youth programmes under the European Union, the Council of Europe, the Commonwealth and the United Nations and with countries on the Pacific Rim.

We also wish to see a transnational component to all aspects of the youth policy so that young people and those that work with them can share solutions to problems and good practice together – for example, the Leonardo Programme (for Employment), the Socrates programme (for Education), European Voluntary Service and Youth for Europe.

The opportunities afforded to travel, learn and work outside the country of birth, particularly within the European Union, mean that young people should be encouraged into an international frame of mind as part of their transition to adulthood, if they and the UK are to benefit.

E. In terms of **legal status and protection**, there should be a comprehensive review of age limits across all sectors to ensure a sensible transition to the age of majority. Statements concerning the responsibilities of parents for children to the age of 16, and beyond in circumstances where they have not yet attained financial independence, should be prepared. Where financial support is beyond the means of parents and guardians there should be safety net social provision.

There should also be policies for preventative strategies against the threat to health posed by drugs, alcohol, HIV, etc. and appropriate support mechanisms for young people that fall victim to them.

Developments following the Cullen Report on the Dunblane tragedy in March 1996 suggest that much more stringent arrangements will need to be put in place for vetting and accrediting individuals who work, even voluntarily, with young people. Such arrangements will need to strike a careful balance between protecting the young and not discouraging adults from contributing to their personal and social development.

The needs of young people should be considered and catered for in national housing and public transport policies. Also there must be improved strategies for children in care and emerging from care, and to combat victimisation, bullying, racial intolerance and harassment against young people.

All of the above add up to a wide array of ideal requirements, but these require appropriate machinery for both delivery and monitoring, to which we now turn.

The machinery for a youth policy

Current governmental arrangements provide no mechanism by which the needs and interests of young people can be identified – still less protected – when legislative or administrative action by different departments is proposed. The formal links between departments having responsibilities for issues which directly affect young people are limited; joint action is at least difficult.

Yet the needs of young people, especially the most vulnerable, are multi-faceted. Governmental coordination in other areas such as drugs has shown that effective action can be promoted when there is a clear focus of responsibility and, as required, a designated unit with dedicated personnel. In any proposed change to public policy, or when legislation is planned, consideration should always be given to the possible impacts on young people. Moreover, the views of young people themselves should be sought in a structured way. Civil servants should invariably be required to include youth affairs assessments in both scoping and proofing documentation on policies.

We believe that within Government there should be a minister with an educational portfolio to hold a specific brief for youth policies; to signal the political will to secure the overall coordination of youth affairs and to promote greater alignment in the policies affecting young people. The relatively recent drawing together of the Education and Employment Departments, as the DfEE, helps, we believe, with the necessary connections between education and training as practical empowerment for employment.

Here we have built upon a national infrastructure diagram devised and generally accepted at the November 1995 Windsor consultation; the adaptation is shown as Figure 2. In this the Minister for Youth is a symbolic as well as practical focus for raising the status and efficiency of this whole field. Fully supported by the Secretary of State for Education and Employment, a cabinet position would not be essential for such a minister. However, should that portfolio be widened to include the relevant inter-connected children and families aspects, then a cabinet status position would become essential, perhaps vested in the Prime Minister's deputy or the Chancellor of the Duchy of Lancaster, or the Lord President of the Council or a Cabinet Office Minister of State without portfolio working to them. Whatever, such a minister and the related Parliamentary Select Committee would need adequate research servicing with impact statements and a range of monitoring data. (See Figure 2 page 63).

Given something like this infrastructure, we note that, whatever the detail, representative voices of young people must be secured nationally and locally; ministers and other elected representatives must be accessible. Also, much more collaboration is necessary. Regional coordination is relatively strong in Wales, Northern Ireland and Scotland

Figure 2: An infrastructure diagram for youth policy (3 Levels)

1. EUROPEAN AND INTERNATIONAL

2. NATIONAL

PERMANENT SELECT
COMMITTEE FOR
YOUTH AFFAIRS

TREASURY

OTHER GOVERNMENT
DEPARTMENTS
DfEE
DoE DTI
DoH HO
DSS etc.
(Some rearranging of
pieces of department's
furniture)

MINISTER FOR YOUTH
instigates and mediates
and chairs inter-departmental group

R and D UNIT

INDEPENDENT
YOUNG
PEOPLE'S
FORUM
(Instigates and mediates)

Cabinet Office

YOUTH AFFAIRS
AND SERVICES AGENCY
(executive body
including statutory and
voluntary sectors)

Youth Rights
Commissioner?

Criminal
justice

Care and
protection
(inc. parents)

Youth work
services

Young people's
organisations

3. LOCAL LEVEL

LOCAL AUTHORITIES
(with cross departmental policies for youth)

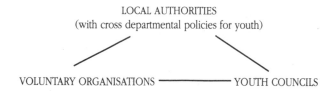

VOLUNTARY ORGANISATIONS ———— YOUTH COUNCILS

but there is insecurity concerning regional parameters in England.

Although we do not wish to over-emphasise the youth rights and entitlements aspect (see that drafted as Appendix C), for we are most concerned with the delivery of those rights by the concerned adult population, Figure 2 leaves open the possibility of a youth rights commissioner or youth ombudsman attached to the Cabinet Office. Perhaps even more fruitfully, a youth commissioner could be attached to the proposed new Parliamentary Select Committee for Youth Affairs.

Implicitly, apart from a properly constituted independent forum for young people, we believe that youth work in all its settings would benefit from having *a stronger national body with a remit to cover the whole field of youth affairs and services*. This body – which could be developed from existing narrower arrangements – would spearhead local work with young people, especially on the important social issues which we outlined above. It would play a leading role in training developments. It would seek quality standards for work in localities. Widely representative of the youth field in its governance, it could act as the channel for funding for specific national programmes such as those to promote voluntary action by young people. It would, in short, offer strategic leadership to the sector.

We believe that to make a national youth policy work, and for the public to become even more widely aware of youth needs (though the tragic death of headmaster Philip Lawrence is already having sustained ripples), major changes of governmental and youth service cultures are needed. This is reflected in some of the comments received through our assessor and reproduced in Appendix D. Over the years frustrating constraints have not only been felt among fieldworkers, but also by politicians and civil servants endeavouring to make responses to new problems and achieve appropriate accountability.

Any central strategy for youth services is complicated by its diversity and indistinct boundaries. The diversity is of three kinds:
- geographical – most youth operations are essentially local;
- organisational – the majority of provision is made by a wide range of voluntary bodies rather than by the state; and
- functional – provision ranges from traditional clubs and uniformed organisations to a variety of informal and community-based work.

The youth service, while having a significant contribution to make to working with young people, does not have the monopoly. It is even less the monopoly of the local authority providers, though the interests of their professional youth workers have sometimes dominated debates about where the youth service is or should be going. A major difficulty in formulating policy has been, and to an extent remains, the inability of such a diverse youth service to agree a clear statement of its own aims against which its performance could be measured and its value assessed. The very proposal is seen as a threat by some professional youth workers. This is compounded by the fragmented nature of a properly, but often fiercely, independent voluntary sector.

Furthermore, what may be described as the non-judgmental and blame-free approach of some professional youth workers has made it difficult to associate them with work to combat youth crime. It may be that an insistence on some unstructured youth service approaches has in the past distanced the service from work to which the Government has more recently attached priority. There is evidence that this is changing, for example from the youth service's positive and successful involvement in the Youth Action scheme.

Towards a real spirit of partnership

Sound partnerships are clearly vital for the future of most youth services. There have been great changes over recent years in the roles and influence of central and local government, and of the voluntary sector. Many feel that these changes have not been altogether helpful in sustaining not only a culture of partnership but also of effective partnership. Rather, these institutions have almost sometimes become protagonists against each other in the contract culture and are in danger of losing some of their distinctive characteristics. All parties have some responsibility for this situation, and there is an urgent need to develop new models and forms of partnership based on mutual rather than imposed agendas.

A plethora of legislation has created a highly competitive culture between voluntary organisations and local authorities, which has mitigated against working in a true spirit of partnership. Yet, as we have noted, one of the main criticisms about youth policy is the fragmented approach to issues affecting young people in their transition to adulthood. The notion of working effectively in partnership must apply across government departments, between local and district authority departments, and between the voluntary, statutory and private sectors. There is clear fragmentation, in public policy and in practice.

For example, four separate government departments have responsibility for four initiatives, all of which can have an impact on the same young person – the Health of the Young Nation (Department of Health); the Youth Action schemes (Department for Education and Employment); the Safer Cities programmes (Home Office); the Rough Sleepers Initiative (The Department of the Environment). There could be a more cost-effective approach to delivering the objects of these programmes if they were embedded within creative partnership. Within the voluntary sector, the competition for contracts, service agency agreements and voluntary income from trusts, corporates and individual donors has now reached divisive and sometimes cut-throat proportions, to the detriment of effective partnership and therefore to coherency in services being delivered.

Young people are not impressed by such inefficiencies, and dissipating competition ostensibly in their cause. We could clearly do better to secure improved NGO/statutory-based partnership approaches commended so often in our questionnaire survey. Unthreatened and unthreatening adult attitudes are usually the best enablers of partnership at all levels to avoid duplicity, replication and ensure that all relevant agencies participate to the maximum benefit of young people.

While here we do not wish to be prescriptive about local mechanisms beyond those suggested in Figure 2, both central government and our proposed Youth Affairs and Services Agency will need to require local authorities to take a strategic view to identify needs, coordinate their endeavours with the voluntary sector and ensure that young people with their diverse needs have access to appropriate services. Effective local strategies can help to ensure that the needs of young people are taken into account by other service providers such as housing departments, and a case can be made to confine local authority work to that of facilitation, efficient coordination, professional advice and inspection.

Good youth services do not imply expansion of state fieldwork activity. Voluntary organisations tend to have more credibility with young people and need a reliable, efficient grant-aiding system. Whatever, local authority duties, responsibilities and powers, like those of our proposed Youth Affairs and Services Agency, will need to be made fully explicit within the needed legislation.

The need for imagination and social glue through commitment

Thus, to summarise, we have in this chapter laid out a generic youth policy agenda and a national structure within which it can be placed. Devising mechanisms to make it function nationally, and down the line to localities, and overcoming difficulties on the way is in reality to do with implementation and goodwill, details of which it is not proper for us to comment on. We see an essentially supportive mix of 'top-down' and 'bottom-up' approaches, with mutual recognition of creative ideas and accountabilities. *The core goals are capability building, social inclusion and citizen formation of all our young people as an expression of democracy.*

Involved for many of us is a leap of imagination to get 'inside the shoes' of our young people, including their sense of justice and idealism. Such 'mind reading' is the core condition for connecting with them to assist in their full formation, as all those who work effectively with young people know. The consequences of such mind-reading are almost always reciprocal if we are patient enough.

But there is and will be an increasingly high potential price to be paid on any temptations towards adult difference.

The social and moral glue required by any functioning society includes, crucially, an understanding or compact between no less than three generations: children and youth, mid-phase adults and senior citizens. Life course phases of human development and the need for social and cultural survival, whatever the context, dictate this truism. This is implicit in the evolved behaviour, including ritual, of human societies, rather than necessarily written in contractual terms. Nonetheless, there has to be a contract between generations to fulfil dependency care (particularly for infants, children, the frail elderly and the disabled), and to distil and hand on accrued wisdom for both survival and life enhancement.

In Chapter 3 we noted that an important phase in securing this intergenerational necessity is the safe transition of the physically mature, but psychologically immature adolescent to young responsible adult citizen. Societies with a future ensure that a high proportion of these transitions are successful as multidimensional rites of passage.

Adolescents and young adults who are or feel markedly disenfranchised of nurture or participation, or both, have the capability of causing significant social and community unrest viewed far wider than crime.

Social unrest can be observed largely as bad behaviour. More wisely we can look upon it as the almost inevitable consequence of multiple frustrations born for critical mass groups or loners out of:

- misjudged 'political' priorities, taking mutual nurture for granted;
- inadequate neighbourhood environments and stressed upbringing;
- locally high unemployment;
- wealth and opportunity gaps known as too wide;
- insufficiently relevant and stimulating education; and
- lack of trustworthy leadership, with goals seen as ethical and fair with leader behaviour sufficiently to match.

Such social justice frustrations prompt feelings of powerlessness, hopelessness, relative isolation and marginalisation. These feed quite naturally the more fundamental emotions of both hunger and anger. These emotions, if unassuaged by appropriate intervention, can readily trigger breakdowns in social relations and social order which civic authorities cannot ignore.

Whatever the response at that stage, it becomes costly on a range of dimensions. Unresolved, unmediated conflict generally has such repercussions, sometimes more enhanced among the young whose emotional controls are often less 'mature' and more socially obtrusive.

We fear that if society continues its current, at best half-hearted youth policy approach, both the risks and the losses are too great to contemplate.

In that light our recommendations now presented have considerable ethical and practical force, demanding firstly a piercing of the thick armour of indifference and distancing from children and youth which we have to face as a feature of our culture. Such distancing includes, primarily, failing to invest seriously in parenting as the most important social activity in any culture's survival.

Then, secondarily, at the extremes, excluding far, far fewer of those young people who need the most attention, and pausing before extending prison-style regimes which too often become expensive means of making bad yet unanchored and often practically unloved young citizens worse. Such mind-sets lead to many fatalities, and a 'youth apartheid' can never achieve peace and stability in our neighbourhoods.

Chapter 7

Key recommendations

THE FOREGOING account, new and older evidence and the nature of other reports concerning young people in the 1990s, point for us to some fairly unequivocal and we believe achievable recommendations.

We are convinced that major initiatives for young people are now essential. Leaving aside the imperative of a moral commitment to the young (who have but one life), and hopefully theirs in their time to us as we grow older (having but one life too) we are concerned about a further unravelling of the social fabric, its still later impacts on the as yet unborn, and what will be escalating real costs to the nation of either inaction or half-hearted, incoherent and token responses. Rebuilding social cohesion is crucial – a social imperative linked to economic imperatives far more than is recognised.

We have not been in a position to work out the full implications of what we propose; that is for others to research and debate further down the track. To a degree anyway, at best, any new social initiative is an act of faith based upon the best evidence available. For those who might suggest that proof of results in advance of initiatives is desirable, we would submit that such a demand lies in a world of professional and political fantasy. In this field, more research may be interesting but, beyond monitoring of any new pilot work, hardly essential. Acts of will and new investments are now needed, with sensitive monitoring and evaluation built in on the way.

Our report has built up a picture so that readers thus far will be little surprised at the focusses of our core proposals. These are basically given under five themes. Chapter 6 referred to a number of important ancillary points related mainly to legal and administrative structures and mechanisms which are not repeated here. One of our four themes, a new deal on jobs and work experience, merits rather more extended discussion at the conclusion of this report if we are to be serious about effective transitions to adulthood; in fact it is the practical focus for the other sentiments and actions.

Firstly, we propose that a coherent National Policy Framework for Youth be developed without delay. Furthermore, policy for the majority of young people must no longer be driven by responses to the actions and behaviour of minorities of young people. A framework requires cross-party political support, and secure long-term planning boundaries. Elected members need to recognise that much of the posturing and skirmishing on the floor of the House of Commons and in some local councils, leaving aside issues of the kind being addressed by the Nolan Committee, is held in contempt by many young people and hardly effects the collaborative respectful role models which we wish to encourage in them. This framework should incorporate all key substantive issues in youth policy as outlined, and mechanisms for their delivery, nationally, regionally and locally; we refer readers again to Figure 2.

Secondly, we urge a change of national attitude towards the young to recognise them already as stakeholders. In particular those with influence (parents, people in the caring professions, community representatives, business leaders and politicians) must be available to listen to what young people are saying about their lives – their hopes and fears and their legitimate wishes for genuine civic participation. Such listening, followed by enabling youth participation wherever appropriate, must be an aspect of all key institutional development plans nationally and locally and is reflected in our mapping in Figure 2.

Thirdly, there is an urgent need for far more focused education for responsible citizenship. This we believe should include human relations and lifeskills education, as well as political, legal and consumer awareness, to be delivered through the secondary school and community education sectors with responsible support from the mass media. Relevance to the likely practical demands of adulthood is central to this. In the light of new insights concerning emotional and relational intelligences, compatible methods of teaching in these fields must be applied, and require associated teacher and youth leader development.

Included should be insights into family dynamics and both understanding and skills of parenting, including the handling and resolution of conflict. This has relevance also for the form and content of youth work activities; these we believe should not only be clearer in their specific objectives, but also pay closer attention to building individuals' capabilities in becoming active citizens.

Fourthly, there has to be a new deal on jobs and work experience for young people. We can no longer accept the fact that tens of thousands of young people will end their education and have no employment at all, that is nothing legal to do for an income. Youth unemployment must not remain a yawn-inducing topic, for it involves rejection, loss of hope and much else as we have noted.

However, given even this ethical statement, how might a new jobs deal be created? The proposal demands more elaboration, generally and specifically. So we next advocate *a cultural change towards the idea of employment*, alongside the new scheme of Civic Service Work (CSW) mentioned in Chapter 6.

We do not believe that a new deal is possible on the scale required without a broad cultural reconceptualisation of the nature of employment. Over the past 15 years society has come to accept as fact that full employment is beyond our reach; indeed during that time ways of defining the concept have changed in terms of age, gender and disability.

Leaving aside global forces and technological change, and the ability of machinery to do now so many things for which human hands were needed in the past, which clearly prompt a net labour shedding, society has in other ways socially created unemployment. In particular, equal opportunities legislation and the ideologies behind it, including that of gender parity, and the collapse of the idea of the family wage, hugely impelled by mortgage and housing costs, have pushed up employment demand.

The one dimension of equal opportunity which has hardly been tackled is that of ageism; that is no accident, for it is even more far-reaching than dealing with ethnic, religious and gender discrimination. Our plea for a new deal on jobs for young people is essentially a sectional aspect of ageism. In our society we have reached a point at which employment needs and demands have become hopelessly out of line with the imperative of rearing the next generation adequately and, in many cases, of caring for the disabled, sick and elderly with dignity. The harsh fact is that the safe rearing of children and young people, home-making and the care of elderly dependants is not regarded as proper work, let alone employment. This is hugely irrational if we are to safeguard a future.

We have a sad paradox. Many of those in work to sustain family budgets are collectively away from home and community for too great a proportion of their time, or are too tired or stressed on their return to give regularly enough of the focused time and energy that is necessary for the active care, control and development of children and young people, and also to safeguard neighbourly community inter-relations and mutual service within which household life is embedded for better or worse. In contrast there are far too many people – adults and young people – whose self-esteem is dented and sense of purpose depressed because they have too little or no employment. Though they have time on their hands, they are often unable to use it purposefully in the care of others because of a sense of personal failure. Nobody can show effective care and concern for very long if all or most of their own psychological resources are unavoidably channelled to keeping their own life more or less functional. Low self-worth, loss of dignity and depression can be crippling at any age.

Labour market pressures are tending to push many full-time and part-time workers harder and harder to do more work in less time or more work in more time. There are costs in burn-out as well as the neglect of other responsibilities beyond the workplace. Junior hospital doctors were the classic historical case of manifest overwork, a syndrome which has now spread into many other fields as job insecurity has increased.

Put simply, the employed work which is available is in too few hands, while the home and community-based caring work has often become threadbare, or absent or overstretched. This has direct impacts upon the real welfare of children and young people aside from their opportunities in the labour market. Put in more micro terms, for the intact two-parent family where both mother and father choose, for whatever reasons, to be employed full-time, they risk two consequences for their children:

1 insufficient time and energy in interaction to be effective parents and to monitor the care, control and development of their young; and

2 sooner or later, preventing their own or somebody else's young from having access to the labour market.

For the lone parent family, the pressures driving aspects of labour market participation of the lone parent could be counter-productive in terms of the secure attachment of the child or young person to home base. Parenting by one or two requires both time and human energy as we have noted.

Middle-age has become for many grossly overloaded with work and career demands, childrearing and care of the elderly, with little or no discretionary time for relaxation and civic participation. Among other things this package prompts much marital distress. Yet it is the background to much youth welfare concern, though there are no easy solutions concerning motivation and transfer of load and opportunity between generations. But it will have to come through a range of fiscal encouragements and public attitude changes if we are to bring forward a new deal on jobs for young people.

Nonetheless we believe that something major can and must be done, without delay, for young people to help them forward and as part of contributing to the long-term attitude changes to which we have just referred. Hence we propose that a new flexible national scheme of carefully supervised Civic Service Work be instituted, involving a wide menu of options for young people, and undergirded by standardised living expense allowances. The CSW must have a range of clear and guaranteed options available to all young people at the earliest appropriate time but before the age of 25. We suggest that the full-time equivalent time range for CSW should be between 6 and 12 months.

It is not for us to spell out the detail of such service work but there are clearly a wide variety of community and environmental tasks glaring to be done, and a wide range of bodies would naturally wish to contribute to creative thinking should such a scheme gain the approval of Parliament. We believe that options within such civic service work should include working with the civil services, local authority services, the health service, business and industry of all kinds including large plcs and small firms, the police, emergency services and armed forces. The providers of opportunity must thus be diverse and funding would require general parity of esteem, with some extra allowances made for carefully specified special needs.

For those young people planning to enter HE as full-time students, such civic service work could, for example, be carried out during a gap year. The national scheme would have we believe a wide range of benefits aside from practical and monitored work experience on real work tasks. It would sharpen attitudes, improve social solidarity and civic and national pride. Given well-prepared civic service work supervisors, the scheme would give experience of being accountable within genuine line-management systems and often of working in teams.

Major national resources will be necessary to fund this scheme. Its cultural popularity with both participants and providers of opportunity would increase over time and come to be seen as a cultural and behavioural norm. However, administration of CSW must be as simple as possible; the net costs will be less than the actual costs because of savings which become possible elsewhere in Treasury budgeting. Society will need to consider bearing clearly explained taxation increases to help with the expanding funding seen as a well thought out social necessity.

And *finally* in terms of our broad recommendations, there is no way in which an updated and appropriate range of youth policies can be made to function without some evolving, but at each point carefully evaluated, redistribution of national resources measurably in favour of young people, and parents who are supporting them, if home stability, youth inclusion, opportunity, civic pride and responsibility are to be promoted. This we believe is an inevitable consequence of our overall recommendations.

However, the release of new resources through the realignment of youth-proofed policies, will need to be accompanied by:

- new attitudes towards public accountability by some sections of the youth services, including those who train them;
- increased collaboration and pooling of overheads by many of the voluntary bodies working with youth; and
- a deeper understanding by all who work with young people of the tasks of their transition to adulthood and of methods of learning which will provide both motivation and long-term behavioural impacts.

So there is much here offered for national debate and action. The overall task, whatever young people's backgrounds, is to initiate them into our discourse, allowing them to feel counted as we carefully enlarge their circles of personal responsibility. This is a process of listening, sensitive teaching, joint activity and, above all, of inclusion. Exclusion and detachment have predictable consequences and are both costly and ethically indefensible.

The nation must now rise to the challenges which we have presented. We are far from the only voices expressing deep concern, and we know that we speak for many young people, their teachers, youth workers and parents.

So we hope that these words, the best we can offer given the limitations on us, will lead to action. There are no defensible excuses for the neglect of young human capital. *We believe that we can and must create a new social dynamic and covenant with young people as today's stakeholders for tomorrow's world.*

Bibliography

Allatt and Yeandle (1992), *Youth Unemployment and the Family: Voices of Disordered Times*, Routledge

Barnardos Policy Development Unit (1996), *Transition to Adulthood*

Brendtro, L. K., Brokenleg, M. and Van Bockern, S. (1990), *Reclaiming Youth at Risk*, National Education Service, Bloomington, Indiana, USA

Bowlby, J. (1988), *A Secure Base: Clinical Applications of Attachment Theory*, Routledge

British Youth Council (1996) *Never Had It So Good? The Truth About Being Young in '90s Britain*

Biehall, N., Clayden, J., Stein, M. and Wade, J. (1995), *Moving On: Young People Leaving Care Systems*, HMSO

Bone, M. (1997), *Young People: The Years of Decision – A Statistical Map*, Carnegie Trust Young People Initiative

British Youth Council (1993), *Looking to the Future: Towards a Coherent Youth Policy*

Coleman, J. (1997), *Key Data on Adolescence*, Trust for the Study of Adolescence

Coles, B. (1995), *Youth and Social Policy: Youth Citizenship and Young Careers*, UCL Press

Faulkner, D. (1996), *Darkness and Light*, Howard League

Finland (1996), *Youth Work in Finland*, Ministry of Education, Helsinki

Francis, L. (ed) (1995), *Fast Moving Currents in Youth Culture*, Lynx

Further Education Funding Council (1996), *Inclusive Learning* (Report of a Working Party Chaired by Prof John Tomlinson)

General Synod Board of Education (1996), *Youth A Part : Young People and the Church*, National Society/Church House Publishing

German Federal Republic (1994), *Children, Youth Policy and Youth Services*, IJAB, Bonn

Hodgkin, R. and Newell, P. (1996), *Effective Government Structures for Children*, Gulbenkian Foundation

Hutton, S. and Liddiard, M. (1994), *Youth Homelessness: The Construction of a Social Issue*, Macmillan

Israel, Ministry of Education, Culture and Sport (1996), *Youth and Society*, Tel Aviv

Jones, G. and Wallace, C. (1992), *Youth, Family and Citizenship*, Open University Press

Jones, G. (1995), *Leaving Home*, Open University Press

Jones, G. (1996), *Deferred Citizenship: A Coherent Policy of Exclusion*, Paper prepared for St George's House Consultation, Nov 1995, Occasional Paper 3, NYA

Lindon, J. (1996), *Growing Up: From 8 Years to Young Adulthood*, National Children's Bureau

Malta (1993), *National Youth Policy*, Ministry for Youth and the Arts

Morrow, V. and Richards, M. (1996), *Transition to Adulthood: A Family Matter?* Joseph Rowntree Foundation

Smith, C. (1995), *Young People at Risk*, The Royal Philanthropic Society and the Trust for the Study of Adolescence

Smith, G. and co-authors(1997), *Youth in an Age of Uncertainty: A Review of Recent Research*, Carnegie Trust Young People Initiative/NYA

Sweden Government Bill for 1993–94 (pub 1995), *Youth Policy*, Cabinet Office and Ministries Printing Office, Stockholm

Thompson Report (1982), *Experience and Participation*, HMSO

Trust for the Study of Adolescence (1996), *Teenagers and Drugs*

UK Youth Work Alliance, (1996), *Agenda for a Generation – Building Effective Youth Work*, Scottish Community Education Council/ National Youth Agency

Whitfield, R. C. (1990), *Learning to Love*, National Family Trust

Wilkinson, C. (1996), *The Drop-Out Society: Young People on the Margin*, Youth Work Press

Appendix A

Postal Questionnaire (to youth agencies)

St George's House, Windsor Castle
Youth Policy Working Group

Please complete and return this brief form by 24 May 1996 to:
The Warden (Youth Policy), St George's House, Windsor Castle,
Windsor SL4 1NJ.

Any supplementary comments seen as essential should be given overleaf.

A   Name of youth organisation: ....
     Person completing this return: ....
     Designation: ....Tel no:...

B   **Core principles** which should undergird youth policy:
     Please give key words only (maximum of six)

     ....
     ....
     ....

C   **Current policies for youth:**
     Strengths: 1   Key weaknesses: 1
                2   2
                3   3

D.   **Your agency's work:**
      Strengths: 1   Key weaknesses: 1
                 2   2
                 3   3

E   **Agency's main anxieties about youth today:**
     1
     2
     3

F   **Policy developments which your agency sees as urgent:**
     1
     2
     3

Signed: ....Date: ....

THANK YOU FOR HELPING THE WORKING GROUP IN THIS WAY

Appendix B

Agencies responding to the postal questionnaire

Army Cadet Force Association
Baptist Union of Great Britain
Catholic Bishop's Young Offenders Project
Church Army
The Church Lads' and Church Girls' Brigade
The Council of Churches for Britain and Ireland
The Council for Environmental Education
The Council of Local Education Authorities
Croydon Sports Partnership
Crusaders
Drive for Youth
The Duke of Edinburgh's Award
Endeavour Training
Fairbridge
Friends for Young Deaf People
Frontier Youth Trust
Girls Venture Corps Air Cadets
The Guide Association
Inter-Action
NABC – Clubs for Young People
National Federation of Young Farmers Clubs
Reform Synagogues of Great Britain – Youth and Students Division
RSGB Youth and Student Division
RSPB Youth Unit
St John Ambulance

Sail Training Association
The Scout Association
Youth Access
Youth Clubs UK
Youth Hostels Association
YMCA
YMCA Training

Appendix C

A Draft Young Person's Charter

Notes:

1   This Charter is compatible with the UN Convention on the Rights of the Child and encapsulates the goals and targets of a range of services for young people, recognising the variety of providers including families, schools and the nation state.

2   Young people are defined in terms of age and development, as being within approximately the range from puberty to 25 years, and policies for them should be needs lead through continuous consultation, monitoring and evaluation.

Section 1: Personal value and citizen entitlements

All young people, being of equal intrinsic worth, should be valued and have a realistic prospect of gaining the following entitlements:

a)   Equal access to the statutory education system – seen as responsive, relevant and inclusive.

b)   Assessment, information, careers education, advice, guidance and counselling, and access to a key worker to give support in a crisis.

c)   Access to appropriate further and higher education and training at suitable levels, leading to qualifications.

d)   Assistance to gain employment and voluntary service when sought.

e)   Information about access to a coherent set of welfare benefits and education and training grants which encourage participation and inclusion.

f)   Access to continuous programmes of social, health and citizenship awareness and associated skills.

g) Information and advice on access to housing if they lack a responsive home base.

h) Access to a safe, warm, well-equipped meeting place for young people, within a bus ride, giving an opportunity to participate in drama, sport and voluntary action.

i) Opportunities to be involved in making decisions about local youth projects and a say on other services through a youth forum or council.

Section II: Personal understanding

All young people should be able to understand the rights and responsibilities of being an adult, the consequential relationships between citizens and the law, and be encouraged to develop their own decision-making and personal development plans.

Appendix D

Government funding and administrative mechanisms for youth work

The Department for Education and Employment (DfEE) is currently and appropriately the lead department for youth matters. Following is a substantial extract from a memorandum submitted to the Working Group.

The Department for Education and Employment's Objectives

The DfEE has published ten main objectives. Several have a bearing on the youth service, and one is central: that the department should *'equip young people for the responsibilities of adult life and the world of work'*. The department's business plan for its schools directorate contains a further pertinent policy objective, to provide *'effective support for the promotion of young people's personal and social education by the statutory and voluntary youth service providers'*.

These objectives overlap with those being pursued by others, including schools, colleges and various voluntary organisations. Some pursue the same sorts of objectives in different ways, and others have interests in the same areas but quite legitimately may have different objectives. The department seeks to work in partnership with many other agencies in pursuit of its objectives. A great deal of central and local government resource is devoted to the shared purpose. LEAs, in particular, spent some £281m on youth work in 1994–95, while the DfEE is funding about £6m direct through project grants and youth leader training in 1996–97.

Local authority expenditure

At the local level, the youth service is frequently a joint enterprise between the LEA and the voluntary sector. A major but largely unquantifiable contribution in cash and kind is made through the voluntary sector and by volunteer help, either independently or in support of statutory work. The 'gearing' effect – a small amount of Government money procuring a larger private or voluntary contribution – has been estimated to be as high as 1:8.

A good deal of local authority youth work is now targeted directly at young people identified as being at risk – for example, through detached youth work. The service works closely with other local agencies such as the social services, the probation service and the police. Youth service activities, in emphasising programmes of informal, personal and social education, are often more attractive to young people who have been turned off by formal education. The participation rate among youth cohorts was estimated by OPCS in 1994 as:

  11 to 15 years: 31 per cent 18 to 21 years: 5 per cent

  16 to 17 years: 15 per cent 21 to 25 years 3 per cent

Detached youth work has featured in recent years. It is difficult to compare scientifically the benefits with the known costs, because the many social variables are difficult to disentangle. However, other agencies testify to the effectiveness of well-run youth services that target crime, disaffection and (more positively) preparation for responsible adulthood. Many such schemes are multi-agency, and are designed to increase collective efficiency and effectiveness.

Young people also benefit from participation in the arts, sports and leisure, and social services, whose funding comes from a wide variety of sources.

DfEE direct funding

The department's funding for youth work divides in three main ways (1996–97 figures):

- grant to the National Youth Agency (NYA) (£0.5m);
- grants to national voluntary youth organisations (NVYOs) (£3.0m); and
- funding under the department's programme of specific grants for education support and training (GEST) for youth work training and drugs education for youth workers (£2.2m).

From 1996–97 the NYA ceased to be a non-departmental public

body, and is now largely funded by local authorities through a top-slicing of the Rates Support Grant (£1.1m including £0.4m for the Youth Work Development Grant Scheme). The department is providing a further £0.5m in respect of the Agency's communications work in support of departmental objectives. The NYA's changed status is designed to locate responsibility for decision-making closer to accountability.

Grants to voluntary organisations are designed to promote the overall personal and social education of young people through programmes of work which target 13 to 19-year-olds (especially those who suffer some form of disadvantage, are from minority ethnic groups, are disabled, are likely to drift into crime or become involved with drugs). This funding reaches thousands of young people. A recent Ofsted report confirmed that the scheme had been vital in enabling organisations to develop new targeted provision. Funding was being well used to add value for the quality and quantity of provision. Through the commitment of volunteers and the skill of good housekeeping, even the small amounts of funding concerned were achieving a considerable impact.

The GEST Youth Action scheme (1993–96) has funded projects to divert young people at risk of drifting into crime – especially on large housing estates. Some 60 projects have been funded in 28 LEAs. The scheme ended in April 1996. A national evaluation published by the DfEE in December 1996 assessed the effectiveness of these youth service approaches in crime reduction.

In context

The youth service's work is related to the personal and social education provided by schools and colleges, with whom it generally shares the common aim of enabling young people to become responsible and informed adults. However, the rise in staying on rates may have diminished somewhat the youth service's historical role which has been distinguished from schools and colleges by its informal and voluntary nature.

Since the early 1980s, the department has encouraged a greater degree of coordination in the statutory and voluntary sectors of the service. In the latter part of that decade, the minister then responsible pressed ahead with a strategy of agreeing with the service a set of aims and objectives – loosely termed a core curriculum. This work culminated in the Ministerial Conferences of the late 1980s and early 1990s. In the event, the conferences failed to reach agreement on common learning outcomes and performance indicators. This was mainly due to the diversity of youth service bodies, the local nature of decision-making about provision, and concerns over central prescription.

Since then the department has deliberately taken a less prominent role, accepting for the time being that services should largely be determined locally. It has concentrated its efforts on encouraging both sectors to improve their efficiency and effectiveness. The introduction of a framework for inspection by Ofsted should go some way towards providing a stimulus to local authorities to produce clearer aims and performance measures for their youth service provision.

The legal duty for statutory provision is that to secure further education including social, physical and recreational training and organised leisure-time occupation. These provisions do cover the youth service, and a court case in 1992 (the Community and Youth Workers' Union and Warwickshire County Council) confirmed this legal duty on LEAs. Hence the scope of the present legal base allows local authorities to respond flexibly to local needs. These needs are provided for by a wide variety of local authority organisations – for example, discrete youth services, community education departments and corporate approaches across services to youth issues. The youth service is thus by no means the sole provider of activities for young people.

Alongside these structural and philosophical difficulties, a further major constraint in the formation of policy is the economic context. It must be assumed that, while acknowledging the richness, diversity and value of the youth service, there is unlikely to be any relaxation of financial controls in the foreseeable future. Government expenditure settlements are expected to continue to be very tight, and all programmes are likely to be examined very critically. The youth service is bound to need to bear its share of the burden.

Government funding of local authorities for the youth service is by means of unhypothecated grant through the system of education standard spending assessments (SSAs). Since the grant is not earmarked for any particular service, local authorities can and do spend the available funds as they like. The fall in the 'other education' element of SSAs reflects decisions on priorities which have already been taken by LEAs to cut spending on non-school sectors. But SSAs are not prescriptive and, therefore, decisions on youth service spending will reflect individual authorities' priorities in setting their budgets. In practice, LEAs' expenditure on the youth service nationally has remained broadly level in real terms between 1990–91 and 1994–95.

The department has increasingly used the limited resources available to target those at risk, in support of its own objectives. The GEST funding for the Youth Action scheme, for example, has encouraged local authorities to develop innovative projects focused on similar areas.

There have been calls for a more coordinated youth policy, including for a minister for youth. These may reflect the extent to which, at local level, the youth service has become one part of a multi-agency approach to young people's welfare, and a degree of overlap at a national level evident in the number of Government departments which now fund similar youth projects aimed at curbing varied forms of youth disaffection. Ministers have indicated that a truly horizontal youth policy is unlikely to be deliverable in the short term, believing that youth matters, as in the case of many other cross-departmental issues, are likely to be better handled on a vertical basis by the appropriate departments under the present structure.

There may, however, be opportunities to secure greater coherence in the various aspects of policy affecting young people. There are encouraging signs that arrangements could be set in place to increase the frequency and effectiveness of more structured inter-departmental consultation on the wider implications of changes to their individual youth-related policies.